£orop —4......

£5·00

auttov

M

AN EXPERIENCE OF FINLAND

W.R. MEAD

An Experience
of Finland

'Experience . . . a kind of huge spider's web of the finest
silken threads suspended in the chamber of consciousness
and catching every air-borne particle in its tissue'
(Henry James, *The Art of Fiction*, 1884)

HURST & COMPANY, LONDON

First published in the United Kingdom by
C. Hurst & Co. (Publishers) Ltd.,
38 King Street, London WC2E 8JT
ISBN 1–85065–165–5
Printed in Hong Kong

To all the Finnish friends and acquaintances
whose names are not mentioned in the text, but
who will recognise some of our shared experiences

CONTENTS

FIGURES

FOREWORD

There is no telling where the affair with Finland began. It might well have been a few bars of Sibelius or a few lines from *Kalevala*. Cecil Gray's early study of Sibelius came my way about the same time as I bought the two volumes of William Kirby's translation of *Kalevala* in the wonderful old *Everyman's Library* series. They were found at an antiquarian bookshop in Worcester, rescued from the swollen floodwaters of the River Severn. At any rate, the attraction of Finland was sufficiently strong in 1937 to prompt a conscious decision to concern myself with the geographical background to its foreign trade. For a pre-war student, Finland was a financially accessible country. Even during the war years, it seemed to hover around the margins of experience. By 1947, it was well and truly adopted and, as happens to all Fennophiles, it was not long before Finland adopted me.

And why the chapters that follow? Ultimately, they spring from a dinner hosted by Nokia at Båtvik following a memorable weekend at Mustio on the occasion of the second Anglo-Finnish Round Table meeting. All sorts of reminiscences had been passing through my mind for thirty-six hours, and Max Jakobson brought the matter to a head. Why not put them on paper and called it *My Finland*? I countered with *An Experience of Finland* because I find it difficult to use the first person singular and the possessive case.

Either way, what follows springs from the stirring of recollections of more than half a century. In some respects, it is an attempt to write off the debt that is owed to Finland — 'writing on in order to write off', to use the happy phrase of Ruth Pitter. And if the accent is on the positive, that is because the heart is in it rather more than the head.

The association with Finland has been intensely personal, be it with people or place, print or paper. The muster of references and the roll-call of names could be almost infinite. There can be no ticketing and docketing of references. The dedication must serve to pay tribute to all those who have befriended and helped me through the years. Nevertheless, the beginnings of the post-war association are inseparable from a small group who took me in charge and exerted a powerful influence. They began with Helmer Smeds on a rough sea in an open boat in Vasa archipelago and with August Jäntti in a smoke sauna in Maaninka. They led immediately to Antti and Aino Mäki in their summer cottage, to Nisse Osara in his Helsinki apartment in Topeliuksenkatu (where I shared the company of Viljo Holopainen), to Eino Jutikkala on his 'ridged-and-furrowed' croquet lawn at Sääksmäki and to Heikki Waris (who, like me, had the privilege of Rockefeller assistance) in the old *Yhteiskunnallinen Korkeakoulu*. It was my good fortune to encounter at the outset these friends and their circle of wise counsellors who were somewhat older than me, who were well-versed in the ways and means of Finnish life and labour, and who were generous with their guidance.

In Finland it has been and remains difficult to separate work and play. There has been much stimulus, a minimum of frustration: much exhilaration, never boredom. New interests have led into all-too-many byways aside from the main highway that might have been more academically respectable. Hence, the contingent character of much that follows.

Naturally, there have been problems in writing about Finnish experiences — the spectre of place-names for one. A compromise has been attempted by using Swedish and Finnish forms according to the context in which they occur. Thus, the name of Johan Ludvig Runeberg is juxtaposed with Borgå, while the early memories are of Brändö *bro* rather than Kulosaaren *silta*. Where there are historical references, the name used at the time has usually been employed, though there is not always consistency in the use of Lantmäteristyrelsen and Maanmittaushallitus. In pursuit of this objective, a debt is owed to Marianne Blomqvist.

Just at the time that Max Jakobson made his suggestion, I had been visiting Lamb House in Rye and reading Leon Edel's life of Henry James. The experience of Finland recalls the metaphor of his spider's web. Every airborne particle appertaining to Finland gets caught in its tensile threads. No machine can hold the data of the related personal experiences, no personal experiences can be reproduced as from a data machine. Limp note-books have served to remind me of how great a tract of my life has been taken over by Finland and how much memory is in fact history.

'By far the greater part of what people experience lies in the plane of anticipation: the other plane of experience, memory, is much smaller,' Max Frisch wrote in his *Sketchbook, 1946–49* (1977, p. 266). In anticipation, so much of Finland has been approached with apprehension, which realisation has inevitably dispelled. Memory may be the smaller plane of experience, but it is too large a plane to be encompassed in such a book.

A personal memoir can never be completed. It can only be brought to a full stop by delivery to the publisher — in this case Christopher Hurst. Much is owed to his enthusiasm, expedition and erudition both by me and by Finns at large, because this is but one of a number of books about Finland which have passed through his hands.

Spring, 1993

1

METAPHOR AND METAMORPHOSIS

Fastän ett ringa folk, vår vakt
Mot vildhetens och mörkrets makt
Är mänsklighetens egen strid
*För ljus och liv all tid.**
                    (Zacharias Topelius)

The metaphor rules

The metaphor rules — the epithet too. On paper every country is reduced to a bundle of metaphors and myths. They shift and change in time: they are explored and exploited for different reasons. Finland, the fatherland (*isänmaa*) lies between Mother Russia and Mother Sweden (*Moder Svea*). Historians used to describe Finland as 'the cockpit of the North' because of its location as a buffer between two warring powers. For the statesman Per Brahe, Finland was the *Österland*, the eastern half of Sweden that was the shield against Russia. With the reversal of fortunes, Finland became a Grand Duchy of the Tsar. The Russian bear took over; though, quite independently, Finns had their own myths and metaphors associated with the bear — the Great Bear too, *Ursa major*, Arcturus, the constellation of the seven stars.

Beauty and beastliness have been equally attributed to Finland. '*Finlandia dicta est pulchra terra,*' wrote Sebastian Munster in his *Cosmographia* of 1544. It was a conclusion supported by early British encyclopaedists such as G.R. Millar, who wrote of the Åland Islands as 'the Cyclades of the North' and of 'Corelia, the fair'. The Victorian visitor, Miss Clive-Bayley, found a subtitle for her book, *Finland* — 'Twelve months in the Strawberry Land'. In 1800, the high-spirited Frans Michael Franzén contributed two anonymous essays to *Åbo Tidning*. In the first, the opinion of the traveller oscillated between between Finland 'a Canaan . . . a land of milk if not of honey' and Finland, 'Sweden's ugly sister . . . a land of trolls and witches'. Finland was 'a wild forest', he continued, 'inhabited by bears and wolves. I never went by a furrier's without shivering a little at the thought of Finland.'

The second essay purported to represent the reactions of a group of Stockholmers on hearing that the traveller was setting out on his eastern journey.

---

* 'Although a humble people, our guard against the powers of barbarism and darkness is humanity's own endless struggle for light and life.'

'To Finland, over the sea?', cried all the young ladies, and took a step backwards.

'Yes', said one woman, 'I had a brother who travelled to the East Indies. For a whole year I heard nothing of him. The Lord help you, sir, on your journey.'

'It isn't deportation, I hope?', queried a politician.

'Do you speak Finnish?', asked a scholar; 'otherwise, it will be nothing but the trip of a bird of passage.'

Others recorded mixed reactions. *'Triste'* (gloomy) was the impression of Bernardin de Saint-Pierre in his 1764 *Mémoire*, although in his *Harmonies de la Nature* he praised Finland's *'majestueuses forêts: paisibles solitudes'*. A Russian officer, stationed in Ostrobothnia in the 1820s also found the landscape *'triste'*, adding *'mélancolique'* as well. The French traveller Maurice Chalhoub identified Finland as *'lointaine et rêveuse . . . mélancolique et incertaine'*. His countryman Xavier Marmier had earlier, in 1863, proclaimed Finland to be 'a Newfoundland discovered by the genius of commerce' with 'commercial jargon' in Turku (Åbo) 'vibrating from one end of the table to the other'. In Helsinki (Helsingfors) he 'found jokes from the banks of the Tornio mixed with poems by Lamartine, verse by Tegnér and the latest news from the Neva'. In his *Letters from London* (1862), Zacharias Topelius recorded a conversation overheard at 'the Great Exhibition: *'Dieses Finnland es ist ja so ein klein Ländchen, nicht wahr?'* — and the response, *'Oh, ein ganz unbedeutendes Ländchen: ungefähr wie Preussen, Bayern und Württemberg zusammengenommen'*.

Geographically, Finland has long been 'the land of lakes' . . . of 10,000 lakes. And now, with new mechanical methods of counting, the number of those exceeding one hectare has been lifted to fully 50,000. The lakes are complemented by forests — forests breeding their own metaphors and symbols, generating their own vocabulary, perhaps inducing their own mentality. The coniferous stands are described as dark, harbouring the forest god Tapiola: the waters that they surround are also dark, the waters of Tuonela. Jean Sibelius projected both Tapiola and Tuonela in a minor key. The prophetic vignette of Sibelius by Charles Baudelaire introduced other adjectives. *'A travers la fumée de son cigare, il regard l'horizon sinistre et brumeux'*. He was not alone in attributing sinister and sombre qualities to the mood of the Finnish landscape.

Northerliness is another indisputible characteristic. The map confirms the title of the book by Eugene van Cleef — *Finland, the Republic farthest North* (1929), which many years later was discussed with him in Bloomington. For the author Hugo Ekhammar, Finland is 'the land trapped in the north' (*det nordfångna landet*): for Shelley, northerliness was equated with infertility — 'the unmaternal bosom of the north'. Not surprisingly, 'north' — *pohjola* — is a word central to Finnish language and thought.

Nor does the grid of longitude, which indicates Finland's easterly location, offer a corrective to the image. It defines a land withdrawn from the ameliorating influence of the western ocean. For West Europeans, Finland is 'a part of the west in the east': for Russians, 'a stepson of the west'. Add north to east and it would seem that, in the phrase of the poet John Donne, the isolation of Finland reduces it to one of the 'suburbs of the Old World'.

In the past, geographical location has been a primary cause of poverty — restricting agricultural opportunity and food supply, inhibiting trade because of the distance from markets. Poverty is a theme running through Finnish history and literature. Times of famine recur in the records kept by parish priests in the church registries: times of feasting have a subordinate place. H.G. Porthan in his *Geography of Finland* (1795) identified famine as one of the scourges regularly afflicting his country. Poverty enters into the first verse of J.L. Runeberg's poem *Vårt land* — 'Our land is poor for those who seek but gold '.

The adjective 'poor' was attached to Finland by the English-speaking world during the Winter War, when 'poor' (in the sense of helplessness rather than of poverty) was juxtaposed with the diminutive 'little'. Finland became 'poor little Finland', the Finns 'poor little Finns'. Territorially speaking, the United Kingdom was smaller than Finland at the time, although the Finnish population of less than 5 million could have been accounted 'little'.

Finns were also long confused with Lapps, whose stature was regularly described as 'little'. The confusion was not helped by either Sara Wacklin from Oulu, who was known as 'the Lapp Woman' in Second Empire Paris, or by Frans Michael Franzén, who on arriving in the same city on Fructidor 18 facetiously introduced himself as *'un voisin des Lapons'*. The witchcraft associated with Lapps was also transferred to Finns, with the result that sinister qualities have been ascribed to a disproportionate number of Finnish characters in fictional literature. In fact, the Lapps (Same, as they are now called) are treated by the outside world as wholly exotic figures in a sub-Arctic landscape, are exploited by the contemporary tourist trade and are accorded attention out of all proportion to their numbers or their wishes. Not surprisingly, they have begun to turn the tables, stressing their minority rights. They have been produced their own flag and their own map — Lapland-centred, a Scandinavia turned upside down, employing their own nomenclature.

Finland itself has been very map-minded. Maps were being used at the end of the nineteenth century to bring Finland to the attention of the world academic community. At the sixth International Geographical Congress held in London in 1895, Finnish delegates displayed sixty-three maps of various aspects of their country's geography. Shortly after, the Finnish

Geographical Society produced the world's first national atlas. It was gratifying in 1992 to be able to congratulate the hard-working friends whose decade of research brought into being the fifth edition of the *Atlas of Finland*, an ambitious project which summarises in its twenty-six folios every aspect of the country's physical and human geography. The *Atlas* is a cartographic encyclopaedia which is calculated to correct misunderstandings and misrepresentations of what is still very much an 'unknown Finland'.

Known or unknown, in an age given to classification and demanding convenient reference at the international level, all countries tend to be slotted into regional collectivities. It has been interesting to see the changing treatment of Finland, for — although Finns would have it so — Finland cannot simply be Finland. The epithet 'the fifth Scandinavian state' was coined by outsiders in the inter-war years, but Finns were reluctant to accept the appelation 'Scandinavian'. In the eyes of the outside world, Finland was consequently referred to at best as 'the odd man out' in the family of Scandinavian nations: at worst, as a satellite of the U.S.S.R. and therefore one of the east European states. The search for a collective noun acceptable to the five countries led to the adoption of 'Norden' which, despite the objections of philological purists, is still used among the five although it has never been widely adopted outside. Happily, with the slow disappearance of the pejorative associations suffered by the adjective 'Nordic' and with the creation of the Nordic Council in 1952 and Finland's adherence to it in 1956, the way was open for the international acceptance of 'the Nordic Countries', with Finland as an integral part.

Simultaneously, Finland has had to be fitted into the typologies of political scientists. Thus, in the typology of Anthony Giddens, Finland falls between the 'peripherally aligned' and the 'peripherally non-aligned' states — a position outmoded by the events of 1989.

All such groupings are of concern to Finns because they affect the international image of their country. There is sensitivity about the form that these external impressions take and the ways in which they emerge. Accordingly, embassy representatives have come into being to keep an eye on the image of their homeland. Surveys and seminars discuss the character of the myths that exist and how errors can be corrected. Cynics have come to regard the publicity machine that results as an aspect of 'the Finnish masochism industry'.

Finland is not unique in that the ghosts of its past haunt the present for far too long. In the West European schoolroom during the days before the information revolution, it used to take as long as two decades before changes of basic information about other lands found their way into textbooks. It is a process which cannot be hastened. The time-lag is an equally critical factor in the export trade. In the United Kingdom, for example, it took about a generation for Swedish products to acquire their reputation for high quality. Virtually identical Finnish goods may be of equal quality, but the market has been slow to recognise the fact, often attaching an East European rather than a Scandinavian label to them.

In theory, the information revolution has improved matters: in practice there is now such a surfeit of information that it is impossible for more than a fraction of it to be absorbed. As a result, the information society may even become in certain circumstances the disinformation society. It is often left to television, highly selective in its programmes, to become the principal medium through which the images of other lands are projected. Distorting mirrors have certainly been held up to Finland by television producers. As for statistics, in the collection of which Finland like Sweden stands second to none in range and quality, they acquire an aura of suspicion regardless of their accuracy. Domestically, there is also a risk that distortions can result from the fact that Finns may measure their home conditions comparatively through the statistics of other countries which may lack the reliability of their own.

Sometimes, it seems that there are advantages in being a rather over-looked country 'in a nook or cranny of the world', as the merchant Carl Lindgren of Vasa picturesquely described Finland a century and a half ago. As Finland's position became politically sensitive, the late nineteenth-century historian G.Z. Yrjö-Koskinen preached the virtues of practising an *'effacement politique'* — perhaps an earlier equivalent of the invisibility of a Euro-neutral.

'What therefore is truth?', asked Friedrich Nietzsche. 'A flexible army of metaphors.' And metaphors continue to surround the concept of Finland. Ultimately, it does not matter if the outside world has regarded Finland as a supplicant to Moscow, if it retains the outmoded image of Finland as a tightrope-walker on the Russian frontier or if the avantgarde question its continuing identity in a post-national world. It is more impor-tant that its countrymen, regardless of the upswings and downswings in its economy, should realise their fortunate inclusion among the league of coun-tries with an enviably homogenous society and a high standard of living. The paradox of a situation in which a country disadvantaged in so many ways has achieved greater success in so many fields than others which are better endowed needs no propaganda. It is a truth which can cast aside myth and foster new metaphors among those who can accept it on its own terms.

Preliminary contacts

To have lived through two generations of association with Finland is to have witnessed its transformation. In the relatively halcyon days before the Second World War, with more than 200 Finnish marks to the pound,

Finland was accessible even to impecunious students. The tourist-class fare on *Ilmatar* (2,300 tons) or *Arcturus* (2,100 tons) — 'the most powerful icebreaking merchant ships in the world', as their owners proudly described them — was £10 return between Hull and Helsinki. At about three times the price, the adventurously affluent might await an Eriksson clipper at Falmouth, Plymouth or Cork to sail to its home port of Mariehamn in the company of veteran Cape Horners. Ashore in Finland, local taxi-rides cost 10–20 Finnish marks and *table d'hôte* meals in more than respectable restaurants about 30.

On the smoky railways, burning sulphurous Polish coal or aromatic birch logs, ladies in black satin dresses strove to keep the wooden carriages clean and tidy. It was a leisurely trip eastwards over a bumpy track to Valtion Hotelli at Imatra — an already renowed architectural feature near the torrent the origins of which an English geologist first endeavoured to explain in the 1820s. Beyond lay the old fortress city of Viipuri/Viborg, calculated to rouse tourist curiosity. An excursion to Valamo monastery on a cluster of islands in Lake Ladoga might beckon: so too the broad sandy beaches of Terijoki with their summer villas from Russian days. But the generally undemanding tourists who found their way to Finland mostly took to the small steamers that plied the central lakes. It was all very unsophisticated — 'away from it all', in the words of the Victoria Street travel agent who handled British enquiries.

Eastwards a virtually closed Russian frontier forced Finland to look west. Westwards, Finland found its principal market in the United Kingdom, with deal boards and pitprops, plywood, paper and newsprint having their landfall at thirty or forty different harbours. Southwards, beyond the shining summer waters of the Baltic Sea (ambiguously, the East Sea to Finns), lay an energetic Germany, principal origin of Finland's technical expertise, source of inspiration for Finland's Lutheran church, a land which had helped Finland to consolidate the independence that Lenin underwrote in January 1918. Northwards, beyond seemingly endless forests and a network of dirt roads, lay the Lapland fells and the long corridor of land that led between Russia and Norway, past the nickel deposits which Canadian Nickel Mond had already acquired, to the small settlement of Liinahamari on the Arctic Ocean. It was territory sufficiently remote to attract the British Public Schools Exploration Society at the time, as a result of which some of its members retained a life-long attachment to Finland.

For a visitor Finland felt foreign in a way that the Scandinavian countries did not. Perhaps this was due to the sound of the language and even more to its sight in print. Somehow, Finland was not quite Western Europe; yet, for all the rural simplicity, it differed from the other agrarian states of Eastern Europe. Like them, so many of its country people seemed to retain 'the open mind of the innocent' (to steal a phrase from Gertrude Himmelfarb). Unlike them, its owner-operating farmers could scarcely be called 'peasant', although the word was regularly used of them in most English language literature and lingered in most pre-war encyclopaedias. Following in the footsteps of the Finnish rural sociologist Hannes Gebhardt, the Danish economist Thorsten Odhe subtitled his book on Finland 'a nation of cooperators'.

In a way, the subtitle was ironic. Accurate though it might be in describing the day-to-day management of the dominantly farming economy, it concealed as much as it revealed. A variety of tensions lay beneath the surface over which the unsuspecting visitor might stumble. There were sharp political divisions between left and right. The bitter legacy of Red and White from the Civil War persisted. (How does one recharge a conversation the flow of which has been interrupted by the startling comment 'Oh, so you have met her — her brother shot my father', and, many years later, react on being shown the place at the family farm where he fell?) The antipathy between Swedish-speaking and Finnish-speaking Finns is recalled. At student parties in London in 1938, they tended to segregate themselves at opposite ends of a room. There was also the legacy of the experiment with prohibition, making for social division between those who drank alcohol and those who regarded it as sinful. And division of opinion tended to run to extremes. Although the visitor was not aware of it, the community of Finnish communities was held together in uneasy equilibrium.

Externally, there was the uneasy equilibrium of the international situation, though within it were seeds that were calculated to unify the nation and reduce if not eliminate its internal tensions. Finland was already being regarded as a possible springboard for Germany against Leningrad in the event of a future European conflict. And yet, as one of the successor states born out of the Versailles settlement, Finland was at least as stable as any of the others. It was also to prove as vulnerable as any; but uniquely resistant and resilient.

In the United Kingdom, Finland was largely a *terra incognita*. The historian J. Hampden Jackson had written the best available book in English on Finland from his retreat outside Cambridge. R.A. Burnham was listed as an honorary lecturer in Finnish in the calendar of the University of London. The name of Edward Westermarck rang bells among anthropologists, and Tancred Borenius was known as a distinguished art critic. There was a small Anglo-Finnish Society, closely linked with Hambros Bank, which blossomed at the time of its occasional dinners. Diplomatic circles were impressed by a Finnish Minister whose Lancastrian wife was a highly successful hostess. They were to prove the right couple in the right place at the right time. A small church at the southern end of

the Rotherhithe Tunnel in south-east London catered for the needs of the
Finnish sailors whose ships crowded the Surrey Docks. There was a
Finnish section of the London Chamber of Commerce, with a solitary shelf
of Finnish material. The music of Sibelius had come of age.

It was, however, a score or so of old-established trading companies
which were at the heart of London's Finnish connection. They were run
by a minor aristocracy of merchants, subtly hierarchical in their individual
relationships, but all of whom had close personal contacts with their
Finnish counterparts. Some traders, such as Neame and Company, had
connections going back to the end of the eighteenth century (as Sakari
Virtanen discovered when writing his history of the Kemi Company).
Others, such as Price and Pierce, the history of which was commissioned
but never completed, owed much to the personalities of individual direc-
tors. Among them was Henry McGrady Bell, who had been the first
political representative sent by the Foreign Office to independent Finland
in 1919, and who became the first Finnish Consul General in London. He
contributed to Anglo-Finnish commercial understanding by arranging for
young company recruits to have work experience in provincial factories in
Finland where they were expected to learn something of the languages,
and where they inevitably struck up lasting friendships with their opposite
numbers. His autobiography *Land of Lakes* (1950) contains many intimate
inter-war war glimpses of Finland. During the Winter War of 1939–40,
he devoted his organisational talents to The Finland Fund, which was set
up to help the Finnish Red Cross.

Never were so many pages of the world's press devoted for so long to a
small country as to Finland during the three months of the Winter War.
(Never were so many volumes of Finnish memoirs published as at the
fiftieth anniversary of the conflict — *trois seuls mois et un siècle de
souvenirs*.) As far as they can be, the causes and consequences of the Winter
War must by now have been unravelled. The war 'in a land where White
is only snow/And Red is only blood' (as Graham Greene described it in a
poem to the *Spectator*) elicited a remarkable response in Western Europe. In
the United Kingdom, passions were aroused by the Russophiles, led by the
lawyer and publicist D.N. Pritt, who pointed an adversarial finger at an
aggressive Finland. A cross-party delegation was sent by the British government to report on the situation. It resulted in a day-by-day diary from
the trade unionist Walter Citrine, which Penguin Books contrived to
publish within a few weeks. Until the end of hostilities in Finland in
March 1940, the war on the western front claimed fewer headlines. Many
years later, memories of Bo Carpelan's 'small country glowing by itself in
the darkness' yielded perceptive paragraphs in Harold Macmillan's
memoirs. Strange symbols are recalled — Macmillan's white fur hat
which he had been given by Mannerheim and which he subsequently wore

in Moscow, the Russian helmet and Karelian leather kneeboot loaned to Francis Noel-Baker by his father and in which money for the Finnish Red Cross was collected in Cambridge Market Square.

Half a century later, when about to give the Independence Day lecture at Senate House on personal recollections from the Winter War period, the chairman, Lord Greenhill, recalled that it was he who had received the 'shopping lists' for military equipment from the Finnish Minister in London, G.A. Gripenberg. Perhaps Lord Greenhill could have given a more revealing lecture. Shortly afterwards, Andrew Croft gave a party on the publication of his autobiography. His adventurous life included responsibility for shipping at least some of the equipment by way of Scandinavia.

British volunteers found their way to Finland too late. Their experiences were arduously assembled by Justin Brooke in time for the fiftieth anniversary of the Winter War in 1989. Some supporters, such as Lady Constance Malleson, stayed in Finland after it ended, and recorded life in a defeated country which the world regarded differently in the context of the wider conflict that ensued.

The Continuation War that broke out in 1941 was followed by a deterioration in Anglo-Finnish relations. Personal communication with Finns was severed and Finns in Britain were interned. There was fear for the fate of the country. Excuses were made for Finland's association with Germany ('If someone knocks you down, you do not enquire too closely about the credentials of anyone who picks you up'). Anonymous characters took over Finnish affairs in Whitehall. Friends became enemies. There was an impolite stab in the back when Britain declared war on Finland on December 6, 1941. It was an act remembered when a visit was paid to the home of the Jäger veterans at Porrassalmi a decade later, although in fact the declaration was not made until December 7 at one o'clock in the morning, Finnish time.

The anniversary was recalled fifty years later with a measure of black humour when a Molotov cocktail, such as was made by munition workers at Alko, was presented to officials of London's Imperial War Museum, which has a small section devoted to the Winter War.

At least the declaration of war had the result that the United Kingdom could claim membership of the despised Control Commission that moved into post-war Helsinki. Some reactions to it are to be found in the memoirs of J.H. Magill. Britain was also represented at the final peace settlement in Paris in 1947.

With diplomatic relations restored, Finland made the inspired choice of appointing to London as its official representative a senior trade unionist. Eero A. Wuori was not only *persona grata* with the recently elected Labour Party government, but rapidly established a close rapport with Ernest

Bevin, the Foreign Secretary, among whose protégés was Victor Feather, who became a faithful friend of Finland. In addition, Vuori had the best of all possible adjutants for the time in Antero Vartia. Over oysters, with a preferred mixture of soda and tonic water for himself and Chablis for others, Henry Bell welcomed them to his restored Finnish court at the Berkeley Grill.

Meanwhile the British Council had opened an office in Helsinki's newly-built Lasipalatsi, with J.B.C. Grundy as the representative in charge. The Finnish-British Society, established in 1931, was reactivated. It had advertised for a secretary in 1939, an application was submitted and an invitation came for interview. The modest salary of several hundred pounds a year was to be paid by the recently-established British Council. Such extravagance was immediately the subject of a leader in the Beaverbrook press, where the payment was declared to be a waste of taxpayers' money. In the event, the post was filled locally for the duration of the war. Insight into the daily life of Finland in the immediate post-war years is provided in Grundy's autobiography.

An Anglo-Finnish Society had been founded in London twenty years before the birth of the Finnish-British Society. The initiative had been taken by Rosalind Travers and Aino Malmberg, who was very much a Finnish activist. After diplomatic relations with independent Finland were established, the Society acquired a more formal character. It ceased to function during the Second World War, but a green light was given for its resuscitation in 1953. Active societies linking Britain and Norway, Denmark and Sweden were much in evidence. The model for the revived Anglo-Finnish Society was the Anglo-Norse Society. The Society was to be run entirely voluntarily, with no paid assistance, it was to have no paid premises and was not to go around with a 'begging bowl'. Its ultimate object was to keep the image of Finland before the public. Independence Day was to be marked with a dinner at which national figures would head the guest-list, the proceedings of which were to be communicated to the social columnists of the leading newspapers. In effect, a public statement would be made annually on or about December 6.

The resuscitation of the Society took place at Hall of the Grocers' Company, the master of which, Lionel Neame, became the Society's first chairman. Some 150 people attended. The Olympic Games having been held in Helsinki, it was deemed appropriate to approach a politically neutral member of its committee to accept the presidency. The Marquess of Exeter, an Olympic medallist himself, accepted the invitation. Hambros Bank had held the accounts of the Society before the war, but unfortunately all the records of the Society had disappeared during the war years. The post-war history of the Society, which has held monthly meetings throughout most of the year and which retained its membership fee unaltered from 1911 to 1975, is summed up in nearly forty years of annual reports.

The attractive old Finnish legation in Smith Square, Westminster, where meetings of the pre-war Society had been held, was gutted during the Blitz. The post-war diplomatic mission moved from Addison Road to Chester Square. And then, in 1953, a handsome house in Kensington Palace Gardens (with an entry in the *Survey of London*) was acquired as the embassy residence. Eyebrows were raised at the extravagance, but time was to prove the wisdom of the investment.

The recruitment of teachers of English by Finnish universities was resumed, following a precedent established before the First World War when John Dover Wilson, later Professor of English at Edinburgh University, was appointed to Helsinki. James Bramwell, who had been a volunteer fire fighter in 1940, came back to Turku (his narrative poem, *Sauna*, one legacy). David Barrett was appointed to the University of Helsinki, representing a new generation of Britons who could talk to Finns in their own language. At the same time, another group had their preliminary encounters with Finland. They were the teacher-secretaries recruited to meet the demands of the growing numbers of anglophil societies. (There are recollections of the oldest such society, at the Kalliola Settlement in Helsinki — and of its theme-song being sung as tea was poured.) Commercial organisations also called for instruction in what was to become Finland's first foreign language. It is fascinating to recall that, a century earlier, a Mr Turnerelly was inviting friends of the University to a *séance specimen* of his new method of teaching English with a vocabulary of 3,000 words.

Because the exchange of visitors between Britain and Finland in the early post-war years was small, Liisa Pesonen, then head of the Finnish Section of the B.B.C. (which had come into being in 1940), cast her net for all who had something to offer. Anyone who had a tale to tell about the British in Finland or the Finns in Britain in former times was a welcome catch. Old travel books had an originality in the immediate post-war years which they no longer possess. Since then, they have become collectors' items. Edward Clarke's *Travels* (6 vols, 1810–23) and Joseph Acerbi's *Travels* (1802) could be bought at antiquarian booksellers for £10–15. Others, such as Mrs Tweedie's *Through Finland in Carts* (1897) or Rosalind Travers's *Letters from Finland* (1908), cost but a few shillings. In general, there was a dearth of publications about Finland at that time. The principal forum for serious contributions on Finland was the quarterly journal *The Norseman*, founded by the Norwegian Foreign Ministry in 1945. It was published for sixteen years and had a circulation of rather more than 1,000. The Finns sought unsuccessfully to prevent its demise on the retirement of the founder-editor.

All personal encounters are fortuitous, but within what was formerly the relatively narrow Anglo-Finnish circle the paths of most people concerned with Finland probably crossed. They will have intersected with those of the scatter of expatriates who left St Petersburg at the time of the Russian Revolution as well as with those of the succession of clerics who filled the Anglican chaplaincy in Helsinki. Intercommunion between the two churches was established during the inter-war years and, thanks to a personal bond between Archbishop Fisher of Canterbury and Archbishop Lehtonen of Finland, the ecclesiastical link was rapidly restored after the war. Personal paths crossed with those of Samuel Lehtonen, son of the Archbishop, who came to further his theological studies at Westcott House in Cambridge (and whose home at Vasarenmäki became a regular port of call). About the same time, the son of the Archbishop of Canterbury came to the Turku diocese with representatives from the Anglican church bearing a gift towards the building of a new church at Salla. By the Peace Settlement, the eastern half of Salla (with its neighbouring parish of Kuusamo) was ceded to the U.S.S.R. The old church village was lost and its inhabitants joined the ranks of Finland's refugees. For them, as for others, the time of tribulation continued after the end of hostilities.

A time of tribulation

To return to post-war Finland was to enter a destitute country stripped of many of its assets. Its youth had been decimated, it had lost a tenth of its territory, a tenth of its population were refugees, and an immense reparations programme, scheduled to last till 1952, had been imposed. Inflation was unavoidable. Marshall Aid did not extend to Finland. Moreover, the stresses that afflicted Europe at large in the form of the Cold War could only be exaggerated in Finland.

Survival was the objective. The atmosphere was charged with uncertainty. The reply to a visitor whose parting words were 'I shall see you next year' was 'We cannot even talk of next week'. After 1948 the reply was 'We can only talk of months not years.' Apprehension was heightened by the Treaty of Friendship, Cooperation and Mutual Assistance

---

Fig. 1 *(opposite)*. An evacuation route from a lost Karelian farm to a new holding

Several tens of thousands of farming families were evacuated from the territories ceded to Russia in 1944. No country dealt so effectively as Finland with the resettlement of its displaced people after the Second World War. Most families acquired a new farmstead after about two years: some had to wait much longer. (Reproduced from W.R. Mead, *Finland: How People Live*, London, 1968.)

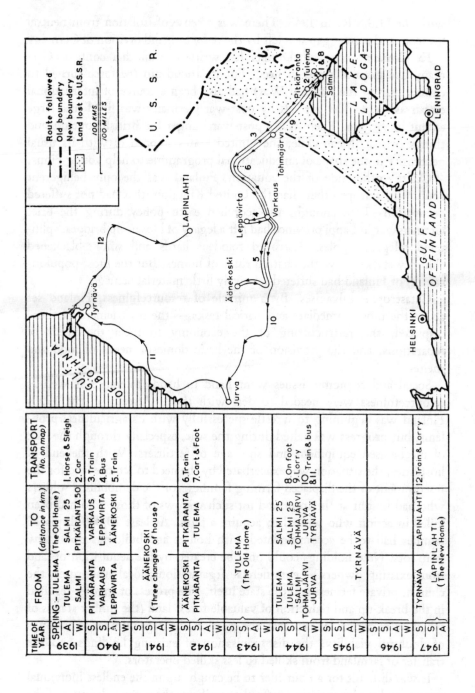

TIME OF YEAR		FROM	TO (distance in km)	TRANSPORT (No. on map)
1939	A W	SPRING – TULEMA	(The Old Home)	
		TULEMA	SALMI	1. Horse & Sleigh
		SALMI	PITKÄRANTA 50	2. Car
1940	S	PITKÄRANTA	VARKAUS	3. Train
	S	VARKAUS	LEPPÄVIRTA	4. Bus
	A W	LEPPÄVIRTA	ÄÄNEKOSKI	5. Train
1941	S	ÄÄNEKOSKI (Three changes of house)		
	S			
	A W			
1942	S	ÄÄNEKOSKI	PITKÄRANTA	6. Train
	S	PITKÄRANTA	TULEMA	7. Cart & Foot
	A W			
1943	S	TULEMA (The Old Home)		
	S			
	A W			
1944	S	TULEMA	SALMI 25	8. On foot
	S	TULEMA	SALMI 25	9. Lorry
	A	SALMI	TOHMAJÄRVI	10. Train & bus
	W	TOHMAJÄRVI JURVA	JURVA TYRNÄVÄ	8.11. Train & bus
1945	S	TYRNÄVÄ		
	S			
	A W			
1946	S	TYRNÄVÄ	LAPINLAHTI	12. Train & Lorry
	S			
	A			
1947	S	LAPINLAHTI (The New Home)		
	S			
	A			

with the U.S.S.R. in 1948. There was a sense of isolation from neutral Sweden, and a great gap was left by the reduction and division of Germany.

Ex Germania lux, Jörn Donner has written in another context. Germany had been a friend in need, but its friendship (perforce turned to enmity during the Lapland War) had also been a source of international embarrassment. The gap left by post-war Germany was filled to a large extent by Britain. There was a post-war hunger for British contacts and things British. Meanwhile, the United States stepped in with its usual generosity in the shape of an educational programme to help young Finns.

On the other side of the equation, Finland was the only belligerent country in Europe other than the United Kingdom that had not suffered occupation. True enough, the scorched earth policy during the brief German war in Lappi province had left a legacy of blown-up bridges, splintered telegraph poles, destroyed reindeer herds and smoke-blackened chimney stacks above the charred ruins of homes. But the most populous centres of Finland had suffered relatively little material damage.

Catastrophe galvanises. By a miracle of resourcefulness, Finland set about the most immediate and critical tasks — the resettlement of those displaced, the restructuring of the economy to meet the needs of reparations, and the provision of the basic domestic needs of food and shelter.

Social and economic issues went hand in hand: tolerance as well as resourcefulness were needed to deal with them. Already in the 1930s Finland was beginning to wrestle successfully with its agricultural problems, but progress was halted during the war, especially through the lack of mechanised equipment and shortage of fertilisers. With the end of hostilities, the situation was exacerbated by the need to acquire land for the resettlement of the displaced farming families, for the demobilised soldiers who had fought at the front and for such widows of those who had been killed in action who wished to acquire a farm. At least 30,000 displaced families had to be accommodated with houses and buildings upon new farm lots. New holdings could only be created by the acquisition of land from existing owners — commercial organisations, local authorities, the church, private farmers and the state itself. The process of transfer resulted in the break-up and reduction of valuable forest land (the timber stands of which were critical for exports), the creation of a large number of holdings of doubtful viability, the disorganisation of existing holdings and the transfer of farmland from skilled to less skilled operators.

It was difficult for an outsider to be caught up in the endless individual stresses and strains resulting from the sacrifices, the more so because of the generous hospitality received from both groups. On the one hand, there were landowners who resented the compulsory requisition of their carefully husbanded land, perhaps won personally from the forest, which had often been in the family for generations. It was sometimes of less concern to them that their land was handed over to strangers than that well-maintained farm and forest were passed over to families with lower standards who often lacked a tradition of care and maintenance. On the other hand, there were the uprooted and homeless families whose misfortune it had been to live on the wrong side of the new border. To encounter both groups socially — even academically — was to become involved in emotionally conflicting arguments and attitudes. The situation called for diplomacy at best or double standards of sympathy at worst.

In many respects, the hardest lot was experienced by the 10,000 farming families who were settled on so-called 'cold farms' — pioneer holdings created on forest land. Most were displaced people who had suffered a double exodus from their Karelian homeland. In the spring that followed the ending of the Winter War of 1939–40, they had withdrawn from the battlegrounds on lorries, by horses and carts, driving animals before them perhaps for several weeks on end. 'Everything was left behind which could not walk on its own legs', imparted a Salmi friend. Following the reoccupation of the ceded lands during the Continuation War, many returned to their properties, only to withdraw a second time after the armistice of 1944. Their retreat was organised as well as possible for a stricken land. Most carried a box or two of personal possessions and a few framed photographs to keep alive the hope that there might one day be a return to the lost homestead. They were shuffled between reception centres, some for several years, before they were resettled — the Kannasmaas, the Ihalmos, the Judins, the Petjois, the Mantsinens, the Sulis and the Kuokkas. It was an episode of which the outside world, too deeply concerned with its own problems, remained largely uninformed.

Meanwhile, for many of the displaced people it was a reversion to an earlier phase in Finnish history. Toil became the order of the day. The observations of I.K. Inha from nearly a century earlier might be recalled. 'Previously', he wrote, 'I had seen the forest as through the eyes of a folk poem — a treasurehouse of the backwoodsman . . . Here, I viewed it with the eyes of a toiler. I saw its gloom, its merciless coldness . . . a hostile force, the foe of man.' The resettled farmers had little proper equipment to harvest the timber that had been allotted to them. With axe, mattock, saw and both human and animal labour they sought to clear as much as possible as soon as possible. Here and there a tractor was available (a tow-haired driver pointed out where his machine had nearly disappeared into a bog 5 metres deep). A few American Bucephalus earthmovers eventually arrived, only to disturb the cultivable tilth of the land that they cleared or be reduced to idleness because of the lack of spare parts.

To see the operation in the month of October (*lokakuu*, the month of mud) in anticipation of November (*marraskuu*, the month of death) was to view a waste of swampy territory, with yellowing puddles in the stiff grey clay under a leaden sky. Water stagnated in such ditches as had been despairingly dug. Bonfires of roots and branches blazed by day and smouldered by night. It was a living reproduction of Eero Järnefelt's haunting picture 'Burning the forest clearing'. Occasional explosions told of the dynamiting of boulders and stones. The noise and disorder was that of the battlefield. How strange to encounter the observation of the statesman J.V. Snellman about interior Finland during the days of his youth — 'where there are forests, there is misery'.

The emerging 'cold farms' were seen at close quarters in northern Savo and in the Kemi valley. A hectare of parsimonious tillage might be won after a year of effort. Their earthbound owners, growing old before their time, became grey like the podsol soils. A decade of struggle with the wilderness had to pass before a measure of maturity was displayed by a pioneer holding. Meanwhile, water must be drawn for man and beast from generally indifferent hand-dug wells. The original cabin, later to become the sauna, was speedily accompanied by a stable, to be restocked (and soon overstocked). Adequate summer grazing in the woodland contrasted with the inadequate fodder needed to cover a minimum of five months under cover. A lean-to on the barn served as a privy, draughty to a degree in winter and the haunt of a variety of insects in summer. Cracks in the planks of which it was constructed were papered over with an incongruous gallery of film stars and notables gleaned from the weekly magazines. Purpose-built prefabricated homes came last, usually after about three years. Oil and paraffin lamps were only slowly replaced with electricity. Dirt roads, dusty but comfortingly dry in summer and frozen in winter, provided supply routes over which there might travel the occasional doctor and the perambulating Orthodox priest (whose churchless parish might assume the size of a small English county). Stoicism and resignation, two qualities regularly ascribed to Finns in nineteenth-century British encyclopaedias, were required in abundance. There was not much fun in life other than that provided by the battery-driven radio, the sauna, the occasional village dance 20 kilometres away, and the intermittent trotting races. A bread and potato diet dominated, but bread was splendidly home-made, even three or more times a week. The whole experience might be summed up in the words written by Johannes Linnankoski in his novel *The Fugitives*: 'How many sorrows are buried in the fields of Finland?' The irony is that armchair philosophers have called land-breaking a redemptive pursuit.

Once the house was built, a warm and dry retreat was available. The neatness and tidiness of most interiors, with their few barebones of furniture, contrasted with the disorder outside. The handful of goods and chattels reached their greatest concentration around the stove. On the regularly wiped floors, socks and slippers replaced the eternal rubber boot. Occasionally a wall rug, handwoven table linen, embroidered bedlinen and towels spoke of a higher standard of living in the old days. Sometimes there was a spinning-wheel. Pot plants might appear on window sills behind double-glazed panes and, with the Orthodox, an icon was invariably accommodated in one corner.

Somehow, for the visitor, the smell of black market coffee was never far away, preceding the appearance of buns and pirogs. Black market tea was brewed, dried and brewed again. In poorer households there might not be enough tableware for all the family to eat at the same time. Among the elderly, there were still some who could recite runic poems. There are memories of a little old lady from Suistamo in a cabin in Luhinsalo, with a faraway look in her eye, chanting a poem learned long since. Before the local school was built, a room would be set aside for lessons in one of the farmhouses. Two dozen youngsters might be assembled from one of the woodland clearings to be taught by a single teacher, who was often a farmer's wife. A dour lady in black is remembered in Savonjärvi; an efficient housewife in Pajulahti. Where there were four, five or six children in a family, the wife of a pioneer farmer was relieved by the schoolroom of a heavy burden.

Life among the resettled farmers and among those who had ceded land was inevitably subject to the intrusion of an army of bureaucrats. Despite them, because of them, the resettlement programme moved steadily forward. Its fulfilment was a remarkable achievement in organisation — and, generally, in tolerance and understanding. Naturally, it was accompanied at the personal level by continuous friction and pinpricks. There were also plenty of failures. The letter of the law had to be followed and there was endless litigation. Officials generated much odium but, no less than the settlers themselves, they were required to be financially accountable. *Esittäkää asianne lyhyesti* (Make your business short) was the unwelcoming sign in more than one local resettlement office. The very words spelt further chastisement to those who had spent months or years on the move.

The hardships of the urban evacuees were different. At least they were accommodated more quickly. Most came from Viipuri, then a city of 80,000 inhabitants. In reception areas, space was strictly rationed. No room was allowed to remain empty, each being required to accommodate at least one person. Somehow, somewhere, tens of thousands of new houses had to be built. The difficulties faced by commercial and industrial organisations in transferring their business from the ceded territories was only partly mitigated by compensation. Some firms disappeared, while others rose more than phoenix-like from the ashes. The old ironworks of Värtsilä left Uusi Värtsilä, a village across the new border, and became one of Finland's largest enterprises. While rationing affected all equally, townspeople had also to suffer the disheartening sight of empty shop-windows, with their cheerless cardboard and dummy displays. They were also to see the fortunate few who had permission to travel to Sweden returning with what were, in the context of the day, luxury goods. Nor could they avoid the attention of the black marketeers and even of smugglers.

Minority groups required special treatment. The Lapps of the ceded Petsamo area needed the replacement of their reindeer herds which had been destroyed during the war. They also needed new grazing grounds. The coastal fishermen of Karelia had to have new moorings and boatsheds and well as dwellings. The Swedish-speaking communities of the Porkkala peninsula had to be accommodated in Swedish-speaking parishes. Some hundred monks from Valamo and other monastic foundations found a home on a Saastamöinen estate in Heinävesi. They were a pale-faced, bearded community, black-cassocked, hempen-shirted in the field, with hats like tea-cosies. They brought a dozen bells, cast in Moscow a century earlier and covered with religious inscriptions, and hung them in a sturdy wooden frame until a new church tower could be built. Their library — more correctly, half of it — was stacked in the upper storey of a large farm shed, beneath which was kept agricultural machinery. In the Igumeni's room, there were canvases of Valamo glinting above a blue-grey lake, a variety of icons, stacks of papers and the inevitable samovar. An army barracks was converted into a church and given an improvised gilded dome. (In happier times a pilgrim church replaced it, while the treasures of the old island monastery were elevated to glass cases in the Orthodox Museum at Kuopio.)

Within the constraints of time and place, Finland probably succeeded in dealing with its refugee problem more successfully than any other war-torn country: so, too, with the rehabilitation of its armed forces. In both respects, planning at the national level called for a combination of theory and practice such as only a well-educated and well-disciplined people could conceive. To an outsider it sometimes seemed that the strain — let alone the financial burden — might be too much for society to bear. It was a mystery where the money came from to support resettled families until their land began to yield a living. Admittedly a sequence of payments was

---

Fig. 2 *(opposite)*. The story of six pioneer farms

It has been a memorable personal experience to have retained intermittent contact with a number of Karelian farmers whose families left the ceded territories in 1944. The diagram illustrates the progress of pioneering for six farmers from Salmi parish in Ladogan Karelia. It brings the situation up to date.

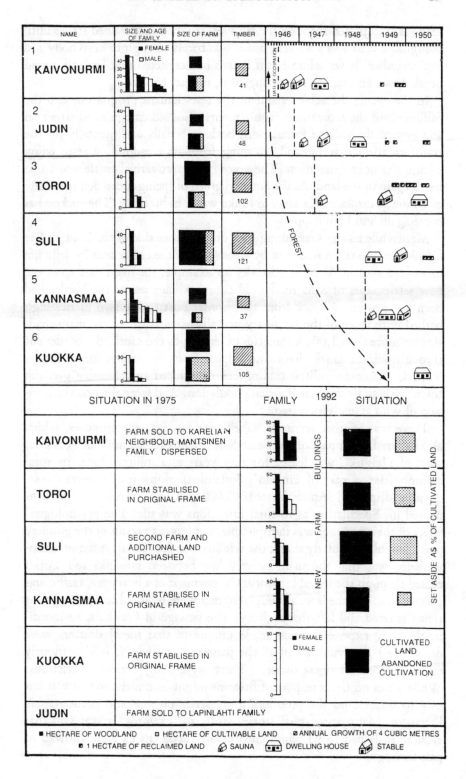

made as land passed through the cutover, stubbed and drained stages until ploughable land was achieved, but it was barely enough to keep body and soul together. It was almost as if Russia had expected that Finland would break down and fall, like a rotting fruit, into its hands.

In the event, the achievement of the resettlement programme and the fulfilment of the reparations requirements absorbed energies and attention and eventually laid the foundations both materially and mentally for the transformation that Finland, escaping from its treadmill, was to enjoy during the next generation. The voice of the proverbial turtle was to be heard again in the land. As the emerald green of spring succeeded the white of winter, a displaced Karelian in Juuka wrote in his diary 'The cuckoo has come again and I am happy.'

Meanwhile nature was taking over on the other side of the border. The invasion of the cultivated land by weeds and of the entire area by wild life proceeded swiftly. Within a decade, for example, the main road from the new settlements of Salla to the old church village across the border had been overgrown. A track from the border post to the two-metres-high barbed wire fence of the boundary was all that was left of the main road. Rather more than 1,000 kilometres of fencing to the south, the border cut through Saimaa canal, divorcing Viipuri from its natural hinterland — Viipuri, the cosmopolitan trading centre reduced to a humble garrison town with an immigrant Russian population. And from the east the invasion of wild animals increased.

There was another territory, taken over for different purposes, which also suffered. As a part of the Peace Settlement the peninsula of Porkkala, west of Helsinki, was leased for fifty years as a military base. Its rural communities, a part of Finland's Swedish-speaking fringe, were consequently displaced. An estimated 10,000 Russian troops and civilians moved in. Speculation as to their intentions was rife. The psychological effect of their presence was indisputable, not least as a result of the gunnery practice which regularly shook the windows of the capital. A major inconvenience was that the main railway line between Helsinki and Turku passed through the leased territory. On payment of a heavy fee, traffic was permitted to use the line, although engines were required to be changed as trains entered and left the territory. The passage of Porkkala, an inordinately slow experience, was made unique in that metal shutters were drawn over the windows of all the passenger coaches. It was facetiously called 'Europe's longest tunnel'. There were many curious restrictions. While a ban on the transport of firearms might be understood, it was less easy to understand the prohibition of carrier pigeons and pornographic literature. Many apocryphal stories arose, for example, it was said that even animals had to be blindfolded before cattle trucks were allowed to pass through.

In fact, the military lease was relinquished in 1956, and it was a revelation to see what had happened during the occupation years — and what faced the returning communities. Bright blue paint seemed to have been used to the exclusion of other forms of preservative. Flue pipes sprouted incongruously from the windows of many of the larger farmhouses — windows which were frequently and unaccountably criss-crossed with barbed wire. Stables were positively Augean and their doorways too deep in manure to admit any other animals than sheep or goats. Wells were often filled with rubbish. The principal church had become a military club. Strange lengths of new cobblestone roads, laid by hand in the time-honoured Russian manner, appeared to go from anywhere to nowhere. So much bordered on the inexplicable, the more so because to the same years belonged the technical ability that enabled Russia to conduct a series of experimental atomic tests in the Arctic. They were, of course, days when the dispersal of atomic fall-out was largely disregarded. How much more, it may be asked in retrospect, fell on Finland at that time than in the days following the accident at Chernobyl?

'Great strength is generated during periods of misfortune,' C.C. Böcker wrote in the Finnish Economic Society's *Underrättelser* in 1823. After eight years of hard slog, the reparations programme was completed in 1952. Then, 1956 was a minor *annus mirabilis*. Not only was Porkkala returned, but Finland was admitted to membership of the Nordic Council. The recuperative powers gathered strength: the standard of living began to rise. Although clouds of uncertainty piled up intermittently in the east, and although there was an 'official' foreign policy — and compliance by the media with it, the time of tribulation had drawn to a close.

The remaking of Finland

In learning how to live with defeat, both wittingly and unwittingly, Finland learned how to live anew. Its achievements over the last half-century are expressive of a Nietzschean 'creative self-realisation'. In practical terms, the process of change has resulted in the transformation of a predominantly rural into a predominantly urban population, of a primary producing economy into a service economy. It has witnessed the march forward from deficiency to surplus production, from a situation after the war in which there was near-starvation to one where there is need to withdraw productive land from cultivation. Some of this development has been planned, some spontaneous; some has been anticipated, some unforeseen; some has been the product of good fortune; some of sound judgement. Throughout there has been a steady stream of government publications surveying the situation, making their expert recommendations all across the economic and social spectrum, providing documentation for future generations.

Simultaneously with economic and social progress, there has been an advance politically from compliance with pressure from the east (even to the extent of some censorship in the 1950s), through Finlandisation (as the Germans were the first to call it) to an independent situation.

There are other ways of interpreting the changes. Certainly energy, both human and mechanical, has been more effectively disciplined. There has been a reduction of friction — in particular that generated by distance, which has historically hampered contact between Finland and the outside world. Wheels and keels glide more smoothly than in the past. Old rhythms and routines of daily life have been changed: so, too, old pressures. The recasting of Finland's social and economic framework and the willing acceptance of new technological imperatives have gone hand in hand. True enough, Finns have had to contend with new constraints, but in general developments have resulted in the range of manoeuvre being broadened in almost all fields of activity.

On the ground and at the local level, the consequences of change can be visually dramatic. They are equally so in statistical terms. Nevertheless, a flight over Finland still conveys the illusion of a land of primary pursuits — forests, farms, waters in which there is fishing, gashes in the moraines from which gravel and sand are extracted in abundance. In the south, a glimpse might be obtained of a quarry — the palaeozoic limestones excavated for the cement plant at Pargas (Parainen) or Lappeenranta: the formidable nineteenth-century granite quarries, now almost historical monuments. In Ostrobothnia, a turbary for a thermo-electric power plant may be glimpsed. The dams and foaming waters of electricity generating plants stand out — recalling that water power sites are virtually exhausted. As a result, and as if Finland did not have enough lakes, great reservoirs have been created near the Arctic watershed to increase the power potential of the Kemi river system. All in all, for most of the country, unoccupied land takes precedence over occupied.

At the grassroots, it is the change in the technical, theoretical and, indeed, philosophical approach to economic activity that has become so striking through the passage of half a century. The increasing speed of change affects the scale of operations, the direction of capital investment, the diversification of products and the refinement of skills. Natural resources are subject to continuous reassessment: so, too, the policies for dealing with them. Above all, a new flexibility in attitudes to working practices has been demanded.

Consider agriculture. Mechanisation, fertilisation, rationalisation, subsidisation have not only totally altered its character, but have caused major shifts in the frontiers of production. Within fifty years, it has been possible to witness the disappearance around the margins of many picturesque but labour-intensive rural practices — horse-drawn ploughs and harvesters, brown clover and timothy twisted on harvest pikes like wool on a distaff, sheaves of grain tossed on spikes so that as dusk descends they take on the appearance of voodoos. In the Vasa archipelago other primitive practices lingered. Bundles of dried leaf fodder were assiduously collected for sheep to eat their way through during six months of stable-dom. Everywhere, something of the ceremony associated with the potato harvest persisted. Nor had the traditional baking of new rye loaves from the first of the harvest disappeared.

The enthusiasm with which new farming programmes have been introduced has been infectious. Clover is remembered as a crop claiming particular attention. As early as 1848 a moral story was published by N.W. Lundeqvist centering on Mikko Neronen, who became a rich farmer through its cultivation. In the early post-war years, experiments were pursued vigorously at Viikki, the agricultural research station of Helsinki University. A theoretically ingenious research project was devoted to the improvement of red clover in high latitudes. One research team aimed to breed red clover blooms with shorter corolla tubes, so that insects and bees other than *Bombus terrestris* could help with pollination. Another team sought to introduce foreign bee species hardier than *Bombus* but with tongues long enough to reach the honey sacks of the clover. It had already been recommended in the 1920s that only the hardiest red clover seed should be imported, preferably from neighbouring high latitude countries where it had already acquired frost resistance.

The post-war years also witnessed a ley grass boom. It owed much to the doctoral dissertation of August Jäntti of Maaninka (who wrote at least some of it during lulls on the Suomussalmi front in the war). The diffusion of ensiling, based on the Finnish method of A.I. Virtanen, ran hand in hand with the improvement of ley crops. Simultaneously, programmes of deep drainage were encouraged, not only to extend the field area but also to reduce weed growth.

Meanwhile, much excitement was generated by the advance of the frontiers of grain cultivation north of the Arctic circle — this against the background of new hybrid seeds. Changes in animal husbandry ran in parallel. Dairy cattle were improved through the purchase of pedigree bulls by cooperative societies, with artificial insemination widely extending the range of their operations. The practice offered special advantages to small-holders in thinly peopled areas. The face of the countryside was also changed through the rise of model farm buildings, increasingly produced as standardised pre-fabricated units, with pumped and piped water.

In its early stages, mechanisation could only ease the lot of the well-to-do farmer, so that in the inter-war years most of the farming fraternity still relied on horsepower. The reduction in the price of machinery, the production of small-scale machines for small farms — tractors, milking machines, combine harvesters — made possible the replacement of manual by mechanical effort. It even engendered its own romance. Evert Huldén already wrote of the 'poetic' concept of the tractor in the inter-war years, although perhaps for every farmer who viewed his mechanical aids poetically there were a score who regarded them prestigiously.

Machinery has increased the manoevrability and speed of farm operations, but it can only offset to a limited extent the fact that Finland lies on the physical frontiers of crop cultivation. The short growing season is coupled with the threat of spring frosts, early autumn frosts and even summer frosts. There are personal recollections of grain withered by frost in the Oulu valley, potato haulms blackened in northern Savo, and havoc wrought by severe winters in the apple orchards of Lindö near Ekenäs.

The post-war years have also witnessed the development of increasingly elaborate schemes for agricultural assistance, not least systems of compensation for crop failure. As an extended country, with considerable variations in climate from south-west to north-east as well as with pronounced differences in accessibility, attempts have been made to compensate for regional variations in profitability. The irony has been that, with all the assistance — biological, technical and financial — shortages in production have been succeeded by surpluses. Simultaneously, with the passage of a generation, animal husbandry and field husbandry have moved from an apparent boom to a slump. Overproduction has called for the withdrawal of land from cultivation — sometimes land the reclamation of which had been subsidised a decade previously. It has led to the reduction of animal stocks — initially the slaughter of large numbers of dairy cattle. Dietary fashions, such as the attitude to animal fats, have affected the dairy industry. Protagonists of animal rights have had a disastrous effect on the markets for Finland's highly successful fur farming industry — and on what promised to be the world's largest fur auction in the immense new premises at Vantaa.

In Finland, farming and forestry have always gone hand in hand. By the 1950s agromania was already accompanied by silvamania. This development was inseparable from the rising price of softwoods which eliminated the so-called 'zero line' in timber values and brought the entire forest area of Finland into the oecumene. The succession of twentieth-century forest surveys and sampling suggests that with the possible exception of Sweden, no country has a more precise knowledge of its timber stock both quantitatively and qualitatively. Silvicultural policy is geared to maximising yields. Experimental wood lots and large-scale programmes are equally relevant. There are memories of visiting a timber stand in Yli-Tornio (complete with a veil for protection against mosquitoes) where hundreds of plastic bags had been tied to individual fir-cones with the object of collecting the best possible seed material. At the national level drainage has commanded attention, not least of peatlands which are potential areas of softwood colonisation. Fertilisers have had their advocates. There are recollections of mounds of fertiliser bags along country roads is eastern Savo waiting for light aircraft to come and distribute their contents — a process halted when the deleterious effects on lakes became manifest.

The state owns about a third of the nation's forests, mostly in the north where extensive areas of poor quality and formerly unsaleable timber have been systematically burnt over and re-seeded. It was strange in the second half of the twentieth century to see the historic practice of swidden writ large over entire hillsides in Kuusamo. However, old forests, poor though they may be for commercial timber, provide in their ground cover the best winter pastures for reindeer, so further tension has been created between a traditional way of life and a new practice. The conflict has been sharpened with the intensification of atmospheric pollution, in particular from across the Russian border. Foresters argue that in this fragile physical environment young plantations withstand its effects better than ancient woodlands. The damage rising from toxic emissions, the methods for combating them and the theories for assessing their impact all belong to the agenda of the new generation of silviculturalists.

Another objective of far-sighted forest administrators has been to improve productivity through education, especially for the multitude of owners. It was instructive to be present at the opening of the first forestry school for smallholders at Toivala and to join with the first students as they engaged in their practical fieldwork. Students attending such classes learn more than mere forest maintenance. They are taught how to assess the value of timber, how and when to sell, and how to collaborate with neighbours where properties are fragmented, as they so often are. They are given new insights into forestry and stand in contrast to the increasing number of urban forest owners who are concerned primarily with investment.

Other changes have been witnessed. The explosion of forest technology, from mechanised planting, through felling and transporting, has converted foresty into a skilled occupation and very substantially reduced the seasonal demand for unskilled labour. Simultaneously, there have been changes in the language of forestry. On the managerial and research side, so much activity is reduced to a series of formulae. It is a healthy corrective that large numbers of academic foresters and industrial executives own forest lots or have woodland in the family, so that their theory is unlikely to be divorced from practice. New vocabularies have also been spawned at the international level, causing headaches for those who have to find Finnish equivalents. It has been interesting to see the emergence of a whole range of new concepts, from the simple ecosytem, through biomass and energy flow, to the genetic elasticity of trees. To attend international forestry congresses is to see the respect in which Finland is held. Through their experience and experiments, not forgetting the empathy between them and their woodlands, Finns have made major contributions to the understanding of timber in general and that of the boreal forest in particular.

The regularly threatened shortfall of softwood supplies, offset by imports from Russia, has turned attention to hardwood stocks. The birch, once dubbed the bamboo of Finland because of the variety of uses to which it can be put — from *tuohityöt* or birchbark work to sauna switch, from veneers and plywoods to elaborate laminates — has been brought into the pulping process. Thus, Enso-Gutzeit, with its elaborate production mix, has a special unit devoted to birch pulp, located in a generous procurement area on the Russian border.

With the rationalisation of forestry, something of the picturesque — perhaps, more correctly, the superficially picturesque — has disappeared. The loggers and their legends have been largely reduced to public entertainers at summer logging races. There is no longer the massive migration of Ostrobothnian lumberjacks with their horses to the northern woodlands. Increasingly strict regulations govern winter encampments and the mobile caravanserais from which teams operate today.

It has been a remarkable experience to have observed the decline of employment in agriculture and forestry to 10 per cent of the Finnish labour force. It was difficult to believe that during the first post-war generation, metallurgy and engineering products could challenge the leadership of the timber-processing industries in the national economy. The same applies to chemicals and pharmaceuticals in the second generation. Inevitably, statistics show that the service sector of the economy has taken the lead, although many of the services performed deal directly with the production and distribution of the widely diversified manufactured products.

The outsider will encounter the romance of early Finnish metallurgy before seeing the reality of the present scene. The processing of iron immediately recalls the bog ore and charcoal of the Kalevalan smith Ilmarinen. Eighteenth-century Finland also had its modest counterpart to Sweden's Bergslagen, based on local pockets of ore which were soon exhausted. Finnish exports were controlled by *Jernkontoret* in Stockholm on the initiative of which Swedish mineralogists searched the realm for likely ore deposits. Finland was included in their expeditions. Daniel Tilas was sent to survey southern Finland in 1737–8. It was a thrill to hold his notebook, written in a clear, almost adolescent script and illustrated with field sketches (and to reflect upon contemporary aerial survey methods). To his day belong settlements such as Fagervik, Billnäs, Svartå and Dahlsbruk, all of which echo the enterprise of past ironmasters.

Dahlsbruk has its own personal memories. A visit was made towards the end of the reparations period, when scrap iron from the North African battlefields was being used as a raw material — it was ironical to see German scrap being forged into ships' chains for the U.S.S.R. As a completed chain passed slowly before them, a Finnish and a Russian inspector solemnly struck each link, ears attuned to detect any fault that might be sounded.

About the same time, a visit was made to the early nineteenth-century copper mine at Kåfiord in Finnmark, with the purpose of paying homage to a site where British entrepreneurs supervised a predominantly Finnish workforce. Records tell that instruction in the Finnish language was arranged for the children of the employees, recalling the arrangements made by Mrs Finlayson for the children of millworkers at Tampere.

From Kåfiord a first visit was made to Outokumpu, then a somewhat unpreposessing mining town, but one of Europe's principal sources of copper. In later years, the story of Outokumpu made a great impression. From the legendary rocky hill that attracted initial attention because of its glittering vein of iron pyrites, or fool's gold, to the present-day company of international repute that still bears the name of the hill, the experience of Outokumpu is representative of the evolution of much Finnish industrial enterprise. It began with a successful survey by geologists in 1910, passed through the complexities of joint private and public ownership, overcame technical problems, solved transport difficulties and settled down to a vital inter-war enterprise. Refining was eventually located at sites more favourable than Outokumpu. Principal among them was Imatra, which received copper concentrates and used energy from generators on the Vuoksi river. The by-product of sulphur dioxide served the needs of the paper and pulp industry. One of the most exciting experiences in the story of the company was the removal of the entire plant from the vulnerable war zone to Harjavalta, near the firm's existing foundry at Pori.

Harjavalta plant made a substantial contribution to the reparations programme, but rapidly found that the costs of energy were excessive. To reduce them, a new method of smelting was devised. The 'flash-smelting' process is now employed worldwide, Finland having supplied the equipment and know-how for its installation in nearly thirty countries. Since then, new ore-refining methods perfected at Harjavalta have led to a major reduction in pollution.

It is ironical to have seen the name of Outokumpu establish itself in the world metal market at the same time as the depletion of ore reserves has cast a shadow over the original mining community. The search for new ore deposits has only had limited success.

Nevertheless, in order to diversify the economy of Finland's north country, to ease its endemic unemployment and at the same time to ensure an adequate domestic supply of steel, the Rautaruukki plant near the old coastal town of Raahe was initiated by the state in 1960. Rautaruukki has counterparts at Mo i Rana in Norway and Luleå in Sweden and it seems to have been more successful than either of them in fulfilling its several aims. Not far away, pyrites are mined at Pyhäsalmi for the refinery at Kokkola, while the extraction of ferro-chrome deposits at a site near Kemi serves the needs of a successful integrated stainless steel plant. State assistance has been required to save the mining community with the exhaustion of the zinc mine at Vihanti. It was fascinating on a flight to Helsinki to encounter a Sunderland engineer bound for Vihanti to buy rail transporters for the Anglo-French Channel Tunnel — four years before it was scheduled for completion.

It is an interesting exercise to try and recall when the names of Finnish industrial plants first registered personally. In general, Finland is not known for its brand names. Nokia was an unusual name that stuck, having been seen for the first time on the walls of a Tampere factory over forty years ago. Its leap to international prominence has been dramatic, with plants mushrooming in the Nordic countries and Western Europe at large. To have seen the domestic workforce of 22,000 rivalled in numbers by international employees is a measure of its energy. The word 'Nokia' announces itself on London's underground (why not a blue and white flag beside it to make clear that it is not Japanese?). It is familiar to those who read the financial and commercial pages of the European press. The names of other firms have also began to stand for Finland as they have assumed a multinational character — Neste, Kemira, Partek, Kone. Domestically, Neste brings to mind the natural gas pipeline network. Kemira is symbolic of the rise of the domestic chemical and pharmaceutical industries, their status and output measuring the degree of development since the tankers that transported fuel to Finland took return cargoes of wood alcohol for refining abroad. At a personal level, Kemira recalls the chemical plant with the 'Gipsum Alps' at Siilinjärvi in backwoods Savo: Kone, the seemingly countless elevators that serve the huge horseshoe marina on the Côte d'Azur, near Nice.

It has been exciting to witness the acquisition by Finland of the paper mill at Shotton in Clywd and its expansion into Britain's largest. The mill is unusual in that its raw material supply derives entirely from the coniferous plantations that clothe the flanks of the North Welsh mountains (much to the disapproval of local ecologists). It is over forty years since Finns started their regular appearances at the annual Llangollen festival of folk song and dance; they could scarcely have foreseen the present Anglo-Finnish link that has been forged at nearby Shotton.

Paper and pulp have always linked Britain and Finland. Albert Reed and Company (as it was) found pleasure in paying for the sauna brought by

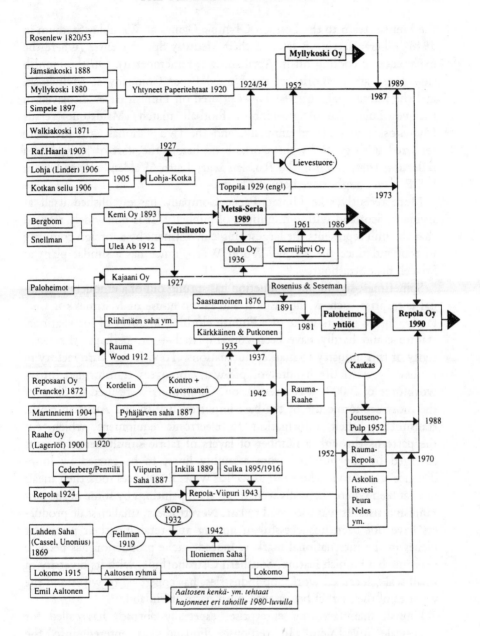

Fig. 3. The process of Finnish industrial integration, as illustrated by the Repola Company

Jyrki Vesikanta has constructed a number of diagrams to illustrate the rationalisation and amalgamation of Finnish industrial and commercial organisations. Anyone who is familiar with the Finnish industrial and commercial scene will be struck by the appearance and disappearance of company names through the years. (Reproduced by permission from *Kehitysmaasta elintaso-Suomeseen*, Otava, 1992) the Finnish team to the London Olympic Games at Wembley Stadium in 1948 and transferring it later to their Medway Sports Centre (where the experience of cooling off in April snow is remembered). On the Finnish side, there are memories of the United Paper Company at Myllykoski and the framed page of *The Times* printed on Finnish paper displayed in the vestibule. An Anglo-Finnish football match (Maidstone versus Myllykoski) was played annually, and the two national anthems were rendered with gusto by the works band before the start of play. And a reflection that, but for the Russian war, Lauri Waldén, a friend from L.S.E. days, might have been the host.

More recently, the United Paper Company has established itself at Irvine in Scotland with a minimum of publicity. It is not widely realised that the mill represents the largest single investment by a foreign company in Scotland since the Second World War. France has a similar plant at Stracell near Strasbourg.

Sometimes, significant production has sprung out of a uniquely individual enterprise such as the fashion and fabric house of Marimekko. Certainly, the rise in its wake of a Finnish clothing industry of international stature could hardly have been contemplated — or, perhaps, the sensitivity of this industry to market fluctuations. To visit the Turo factory in its heyday, with its handful of pre-war employees transformed into a workforce of 2,000, was a revelation. Computers were used to discover the most economic use of the best imported British and Austrian cloth, transmitting their information to electronic equipment which cut the patterns through a number of layers of fabric simultaneously. Suits emerged by the hundred from assembly lines, to be carried by long-distance trucks to markets east as well as west. Employees took their meals in a canteen where the walls were hung with paintings by some of the best Finnish artists. It was too good to last. Nevertheless, smaller-scale producers have not been unsuccessful in finding and retaining their particular niches in the international market. Indeed, niche production has become very much a Finnish feature. Southern Ostrobothnia, with its diversity of small-scale, localised workshop industries, has contrived to withstand the vagaries of the market better than most parts of Finland.

Finnish manufacturing enterprise, especially abroad, has called for large-scale investment. In response, Finland has entered into the international capital market in a manner which, to earlier generations, would have been inconceivable. Again, the Swedish example has been repeated, and it has not been unusual for the emulator to perform more successfully than the emulated. Nor is it unusual for Finnish conglomerates to have their own independent financial corporations. In turn, the financial agencies are linked to consultancy firms. Soon after the war, Finland began to demonstrate its ability to piece together mixtures of domestic and imported components and to develop complex assembly industries. To visit the Wärtsilä shipyard when the market for icebreakers was buoyant was to observe the wide area from which components were drawn. In parallel, Finnish consultancy firms, such as Jaakko Pöyry, have achieved international prominence, assembling information and offering advice on the diverse contracting alternatives for foreign customers. In the process, as with all Finnish endeavours abroad, experience in handling a multi-cultural labour force has had to be acquired.

At home, Finnish manufacturers have become increasingly aware of the limited energy supplies. Only a third of Finland's needs derive from domestic sources. It is not surprising than Finns have a commitment to nuclear power and that the anti-nuclear lobby is small. Unlike Sweden, which plans to phase out its nuclear energy plants, Finland still anticipates possible expansion. It has not only been the tug-of-war between different forms of energy, which the outsider has witnessed and continues to witness, but also the battles won and lost over the location of plants. Imported crude oil has raised the spectre of spillage in the Baltic, especially among the tortuous channels through the archipelagos. Oil refineries have inevitably commanded waterfront sites, and there is continuous concern over their effects on the natural environment. The same applies to the thermo-electric stations based on imported coal. It is fascinating to see the Sörnäinen waterfront at Helsinki, which seems able to accommodate successfully mountains of Polish coal in juxtaposition with evidently desirable residential units.

The energy equation is full of political elements. East and West, for example, have competed intensively for contracts to supply nuclear units. Russian gas, pipelined first to the border and now deep into Finland, is likely in the future to meet competition from Norwegian natural gas, giving the Finns an interest in the development of the Arctic fields. Because of energy demands, it is not surprising that Finland has taken conservation to heart. Consultancy in energy conservation has become a Finnish export on its own account. Thus, the installation of district heating in the city of Sheffield owes much to Finnish expertise.

Social change

Finland's economic transformation has been accompanied by major social changes. Above all, there has been a pronounced increase in population mobility, with the years since 1944 seeing the greatest mass movements in Finnish history. It is remarkable to have lived through it and to have seen its consequences at the individual level. The internal migrations of the immediate post-war years involved hundreds of thousands of people. Resettlement of the displaced resulted in the intrusion of migrants upon extensive areas of the country which had never before known an influx of settlers. In the 1960s and 1970s, against the background of deteriorating conditions of employment in the countryside, a major migration from rural to urban areas took place. It has been called 'The great migration' and was essentially a movement of the young. Indeed, in the rural communes of Finland between 1970 and 1980, the population aged thirty or less declined by half a million. In response to better economic prospects and facilitated through the common Nordic labour market, tens of thousands of young people moved to Sweden. It was strange to hear Finnish spoken in the streets of manufacturing towns far from Stockholm.

In many ways, it is as though mobility has entered into the blood of Finns. Millions travel abroad annually, while the relative intensity of domestic movement must equal that of any country in the developed world. Within the space of a generation, communications have been transformed — as both the cause and the effect of demand.

Side by side with population movement, equally significant biological changes have been taking place. The birth-rate has always been unpredictable, nationally and regionally, but child mortality has declined sharply. At mid-century the young outnumbered the old. Subsequently, life expectancy has increased strikingly. The passage of two generations has also produced changes in physique. It is not uncommon for fathers to look over grandfathers' heads and sons over the heads of fathers. To share a journey by plane or rail with a group of Finnish adolescents is to be conscious of their supreme health (only threatened perhaps by the cigarette packet protruding from the back pocket). Such developments are inseparable from the improvements in dietary standards, dating from the war and immediate post-war years, with the distribution of basic foodstuffs through rationing, and currently owing much to nutritional education.

One result of improvement in health has been the absolute decline in the scourge of tuberculosis. There are memories of full wards at Tarinaharju in Siilinjärvi and of the medical officer in charge succumbing to the same condition as his patients. Since then, sanatoria — from pioneering Hyvinkää to the architecturally celebrated Paimio — have been closed or are used for other purposes. Another result of improved health care has been the disappearance of the large numbers of unshapely bodies, often the product of rickets in early childhood, that were once so apparent to the visitor. Simultaneously, there has been a shift in mental health care away from institutions and into the community.

Basic physiological characteristics change little. However, an accepted scientific terminology has replaced the strings of adjectives that were once used to describe the appearance of Finns and which were commonly copied from one text to another. Whatever the words, it is not difficult for

anyone intimate with the people from parts of Savo to pick out their kith
and kin from among the cosmopolitan crowds in Oxford Street or on the
Costa Brava — the fair hair, the generally blue eyes, the lack of
pigmentation, the set of the cheekbones.

More important, in recent years medical scientists and geneticists have
singled out genes and polymorphic traits that help to distinguished many
Finns from other peoples. Their gene pool has a unique pattern, not least
setting it apart from that of the Lapps. It is equally interesting that Finnish
medical texts list rather more than a score of diseases which are essentially
Finnish — some restricted to particular localities, some unknown except
to Finns, some confined to extended families. Such diseases, long
unknown outside Finland, have now found their way into international
data systems — critical information for diagnosis and treatment given the
present degree of Finnish mobility. Reciprocally, the million or so Finns
who travel abroad each year have carried diseases to their home country
from which geographical isolation formerly protected it.

The passage of two generations has also resulted in changes to social
attitudes. Where there is not consensus, there is often a softening of the
manner in which opinions are expressed. As a silviculturalist might express
it, there are fewer knots in the wood than there used to be. Relaxation is
inseparable from the greater frequency and range of personal interaction.

Ethnographic differences engender less discord than hitherto. 'The
carping language dispute', as Elmer Diktonius described it in his catalogue
of Finnish shortcomings, causes less embarrassment for a foreigner. There
are memories of friends who disapproved of each other simply because they
spoke a different mother tongue, of the sensitivity of being introduced by a
Finnish-speaking academic to a Swedish-speaking colleague, of Finnish-
speaking friends who obviously disapproved of visits to Åland. There was a
measure of bigotry displayed by a Finnish-speaking geomorphologist who
published the definitive study of the evolution of the Baltic Sea in
Quaternary times, but who had never undertaken fieldwork in the Åland
islands, the features of which held many keys to his theories. (In fairness, it
must be recorded that his Swedish counterpart never visited the islands
because they became a part of Finland in 1921.) The constitutional status of
Finland's autonomous province endows it with a unique place in international law, but more than a measure of intolerance persists over the
employment of the Finnish language. Even television does not greatly
help. An otherwise genial Mariehamn businessman is recalled who opened
The Times Atlas and, putting his finger on what he regarded as an error,
asked 'Where is this place called Ahvenanmaa?'

The Lappish minority — *Saamelaiset* as they are increasingly called in
Finland — is small. Less than 3,000 use the Lappish tongue. They have
only been encountered personally around the edges of their territory —

trekking across country in Muonio parish and along the shores of Lake Inari. It was somewhat unexpected to meet Lapp media men in Saariselkä as they were seeking out the field investigator into Lappish life, Ludger Müller-Wille. The Skolt Lapps have been appreciated vicariously through Tim Ingold's studies. It has been interesting to observe the increasing articulacy of the *Same*, challenging intrusion upon their territories and seeking stronger links with their more numerous Swedish and Norwegian kith and kin.

Ideological differences are less pronounced. The extremes of left and right are no longer relevant. The legacy of the Civil War (revolution, insurrection, war of liberation according to the point of view) and memories of the Lapua movement were largely eliminated during the Winter War and the Continuation War. The vocabulary applied to the stressful years 1917–18 is no longer emotive. 'Red' urban districts in the eyes of 'White' supporters and 'Red' parishes in the eyes of 'Black' clergy ('Half of my parish votes for Satan') have been gradually expunged from mental maps. The metaphorically 'stony land where vipers live', of which Eino Leino wrote in his novel *Olli Suurpää*, has disappeared. Red and White alike are but names on monuments — equally impressive monuments. As for ecclesiastical differences, not only the 'established' Lutheran church versus the rest but traditionalist versus revivalist, they cause no more than slight ripples on the surface.

Effective coalition governments, sometimes embracing bourgeois and communist parties, the nationwide rise in living standards and a mass of social legislation have produced a more tolerant as well as a more egalitarian society. A broader gradation in property size and value, together with widespread owner-occupancy, has reduced the sense of 'piled-up privilege' conveyed in former times by conditions of land ownership.

Inevitably, there remain pockets of poverty and misfortune even in the welfare state, but they have dwindled in the course of fifty years. The elderly still remember the submerged tenth who lived in backwoods squalor or in the wooden shanty towns of down-at-heel urban districts. Ilmari Kianto's Ryysyranta, Hannu Salama's childhood Pispala and Pekka Toivonen's Kotka have been recorded for posterity. By contrast it is interesting to reflect on the ranks of artisans' frame houses — First Line, Second Line, Third Line that climb up the hill towards Kallio church in central Helsinki. It is a measure of their transformation that in the precincts of their much improved dwellings are Kaupunginteatteri (the capital's largest theatre), modern harbourages, expensive hotels, Hakaniemi market hall (the delicatessen of which most residents in the neighbourhood seem able to buy) while rumbling underneath are the gleaming coaches of the metropolitan railway. This once shadowy area of Sörnäinen, where social workers began their voluntary labours and academic enquiries, has become largely bourgeois territory. There is no gentrification, simply an upgrading of the entire neighbourhood.

At the national level, as in most countries, there are differences, imagined or real, that attract intermittent attention. There is the presumed dominance of those who live around the coast over those who occupy the interior. In the past (what may be called) the Ionian mood of the former and the Dorian mood of the latter may well have explained their contrasting commercial acumen. There is a further perceived division between those who occupy the south-west peninsula — metropolitan Finland — and those who live in the rest of the country — especially in the peripheral areas. 'Southerners think that they are better than people from other parts of the country,' writes Anssi Paasi. There may be a southern establishment, if only because population concentrations tend to generate one. Nevertheless, there have always been champions (Ilmari Hustich comes to mind) of the archipelagos, the northlands and the eastern marchlands, and the corridors of power have never lacked recruits from them.

A certain antipathy prevails between the farming fraternity and town people, not least because of the purchase of rural properties by affluent city-dwellers who have lost or are fearful of losing their rural roots. Farmers also have their own pecking order socially and regionally. The size of the holding and the generations through which it has been in the family influence the former; the progressive or traditional approach to agriculture affects the latter. The description by a West Finnish progressive of an East Finnish traditionalist quoted by Matti Klinge has not been surpassed — 'a magnificent introverted meditative-vegetative work of nature'.

There is an inevitable contrast between the Finns who favour solitude, the lovers of empty country, and the sociable Finns who crave company. *Noli me tangere*. If Finns want to avoid each other, as Hans Magnus Enzensberger has remarked, they can do so because they are 'blessed with plenty of empty space'.

The passage of two generations has produced an accommodation of differences. Tensions, tempered by civility, can make a positive contribution to society. If, as Lionel Trilling avers, the essential culture of a country lies in its inherent antitheses, Finland is the richer for them.

Greater tolerance has led to more willing acceptance of criticism. Thus, for a while, the Winter War and the Continuation War were too near and too sensitive to permit detached analysis. An official interpretation prevailed from which it was accepted that certain facts might be written out. Foreign scholars who attempted to explain the course of events objectively and in the light of evidence from beyond Finland were immediately confronted with the orthodox version. The bitter attacks on the interpretations of such historians as Leonard Lundin and Anthony Upton are well remembered. A full generation had to pass before documentary evidence became available and the search for greater authenticity could be pursued.

Finland's relationship to the U.S.S.R. has been remotely, but constantly, in the background of the experience of any foreigner. On paper, the formal words of the Treaty of Friendship, Cooperation and Mutual Assistance did not seem to constitute a direct threat to Finland's independence and integrity. In fact, the trading activities within the frame of successive five-year plans built up a dependence which approached a peak as Finland's economy reached a maximum phase of expansion. (For a British observer it was disappointing but understandable to see the historic role of the United Kingdom as Finland's largest trading partner being assumed by the U.S.S.R.)

It was evident that behind the scenes there were pressures about which friends spoke with varying degrees of alarm, despondency or cynicism. Occasionally, for a foreigner at least, they assumed inexplicable forms. The proposal to undertake the restoration of the Saimaa canal offered an example. A generation of neglect could be seen in the Finnish part of its course. At the time of its original opening in 1856, the canal was the largest single capital investment ever undertaken by Finland. A century later, following reconstruction and reopening in 1968, it proved again to be the country's largest capital outlay. Today the 'Friendship' canal has an impressive — here and there even an awesome — appearance. But often the visitor looks vainly for the sight of shipping. In reality, the canal has never carried enough traffic to pay for its maintenance and probably never will. What is more, it has diverted resources away from more profitable and significant investment.

Ultimately, friendship and understanding are the result of practical activity and compromise at the professional and personal level. Illustration is provided by the amiable meetings of maintenance engineers — Finnish, Russian and Norwegian — at the power stations along Paatsjoki river, meetings which have continued for four decades. It is provided too by the day-to-day contacts in such enterprises at the joint Finnish-Russian softwood mill at Uimaharju in Finnish Karelia. It is witnessed in the gesture of friendship from Äänisjärvi inviting Lars Pettersson to return to the scene of his wartime labours when he recorded the Orthodox religious monuments for posterity in 1942–4. There is another instance of it in the pioneering seminar of Finnish and Russian historians held in Moscow in 1989, when Russian documentary evidence revealed for the first time that the responsibility for the outbreak of hostilities in 1939 lay with the U.S.S.R.

Never has so much historical material been 'tidied into books' with so great effect as during the 1980s. Side by side with the increasing access to archives has gone the greater freedom with which authors have expressed their views. No less than in other countries certain Finnish sources remain closed, although their contents may be guessed from the host of biographies and autobiographies which Finns seem to relish. The prolonged self-censorship imposed by the press for diplomatic reasons and the fine balance struck by newspaper editors between discretion and integrity is increasingly revealed. Externally, this gave rise to the concept of Finlandisation — an unappealing term to Finns. With changing circumstances, it has been interesting to see the post-war response to pressures from the U.S.S.R. explained as a process of self-Finlandisation. The need for self-Finlandisation may have passed, but it is not easy to eradicate the suspicion of Russian motives bred in generations of Finns.

The new Russian situation inevitably calls for reflection on the *terra irredenta* of Karelia. The feelings generated are mixed. Many Karelians have returned to photograph near-derelict hamlets and farmsteads where their parents or grandparents lived — the Lapinlahti friends in coaches bouncing over potholed highways and creaking bridges to Salmi and Suistamo and Sortavala. Orthodox priests have accompanied them to hold services in reopened churches. Nostalgia is powerful. For many, childhood in Karelia ran along an enchanted way — for Ritva Heikkilä on the sandy shores of Terijoki, for Faina Jyrkilä around Impilahti, for Oscar Parland fictionalising the fact of the Tikkala estate, for Benedict Zilliacus aboard his boat in the reeds, for the Viipuri residents with leisure homes on Porkansaari exchanging memories of their summer idyll. Some former residents have boarded the *Sergei Kirov* from the banks of the Neva to revisit the Valamo monastery in Lake Ladoga. For Stig Jaatinen, fact-finding on a return to the scenes of his youth, Viipuri (Viborg) was a sad reality. The family's apothecary shop had become a sleazy restaurant, the church where children had been confirmed was closed, the old school was down-at-heel. There was no response to a knock on the door of the old apartment up a familiar but dilapidated stairway. The cemetery, half-emptied of its memorials, was a wilderness.

The social scientist Anssi Paasi has looked at the situation from a different angle. He has selected three generations of residents in Uusi Värtsilä — the new settlement created across the border when old Värtsilä was taken over by the U.S.S.R. Each generation has a different attitude to the old village. The diminishing number of grandparents still look over their shoulders at the lost homestead (for them 'a Russian is still a Russian if fried in butter'). The parents, knowing little or nothing of the old days, are concerned primarily with daily life in new Värtsilä. The young look to the future, which is the west. For them the land beyond the 1944 boundary does not raise strong emotions.

A Finnish miracle

During the years of reconstruction in Europe, commentators spoke of the German miracle. In relation to Finland's size and resources, its transformation has been no less miraculous — and, unlike most of Western Europe, without any form of Marshall Aid. As a small country it did not claim the same international attention as West Germany. Yet, little by little, the world family of nations has become to appreciate Finland's new authority. Swedes have regarded Finland competitively with a certain apprehension: Russians, with envy. Upwardly mobile Finland, as the phrase has it, has made the countries of Eastern Europe realise that, by comparison, they have stagnated for four decades. If a certain material extravagance has been manifested in late twentieth-century Finland, it is only compensation for the proverty endured during the 'years the locusts ate'. Furthermore, material progress has been accompanied by a blossoming in the arts and applied arts exceeded by few if any countries of equal size.

The advance from penury to prosperity is an experience in which two generations of Finns have shared. A third generation, born to high expectations, may have difficulty in maintaining the rate of development. Compensatingly, it is unlikely that the present generation of Finns will have to deal with problems equal in magnitude to those that have confronted their parents and grandparents.

2

THE FINNISH LANDSCAPE

'The true wealth of the visible world lies in detail. . . . Stop a moment at
each and every one, then combine again the entirety in a context.'

(Alain, *Entretiens*, 1931)

Maisema

As its economy has been transformed, as living standards have risen and
values have changed, Finland has developed a different attitude to its
natural and cultural landscapes. J.V. Snellman, the philosopher and consti-
tutionalist, was among the first Finns to use the word *maisema* for the
combination of geographical features that make up a landscape. Reino
Kalliola, one of Finland's leading ecologists, made the word his own. All
people have an innate sense of the landscapes that surround them. Artists
capture them in their highly personal styles — the Finnish artists Werner
Holmberg, Fanny Churberg, Victor Westerholm, Pekka Halonen and
Aimo Kanerva offer contrasting examples. There are literary landscapes.
Lapland is Yrjö Kokko country, Satakunta is Joel Lehtonen country,
Åland is background to the homespun romances of Anni Blomqvist.
Architects and planners articulate increasingly their modes of address, their
methods of inventory and their scales of values for assessing the various
landscape components. For geographers landscapes also generate their own
vocabularies.

A ring in a rock

In a granite boulder beside a cornfield in the parish of Petalax (Petolahti) in
Ostrobothnia, there is a heavy iron ring. 'When I was a boy', the owner of
the land commented, 'we used to moor our boat to that ring.' The level of
the land has risen some two feet in the intervening sixty years. The salt has
been slowly drained from the soil. To saltmarsh has succeeded ley grassland: to grassland, a grain harvest. It is a familiar story along the coast
of Ostrobothnia and it reaches a climax in the Vasa archipelago. The
phenomenon of land upheaval — technically, isostasy — generated hot
academic dispute two centuries ago, with vulcanists the supporters of land
emergence opposing neptunists the supporters of water diminution. The
post-glacial land emergence reaches its maximum in Kvarken, the narrows
between Vasa and Umeå. It is no simple phenomenon. It reflects an often
deeply fractured granite bedrock in a state of flux, with uplift varying
slightly in speed over relatively short distances.

And you granite—
Anointed—
Woke—
Stirred

It is as though Ted Hughes, the British poet laureate, had a line ready and waiting in his poem *Gaudette*.

With the melting of the ice-sheet in the Quaternary period, there was a rise in the sea level which drowned most of Finland's granite shield. The present shape of the country has evolved during the last 8,000 years. Accordingly, Finnish mythology is denied an Atlantis. Striking testimony to the degree of land emergence is to be found in the suites of raised beaches, tens of metres above the present sea level, in the parish of Saltvik in Åland. They are composed of grey boulders, encrusted with lichens and bearded with mosses, and they form a staircase of shallow steps some of which have treads several tens of metres wide. To walk across them is to walk across a page of geological history. It is also to be given cause to ponder what was the fetch of wind and wave that piled up such impressive features. Less dramatic, but no less circumstantial, are the contents of the layered clays deposited well above the present shoreline. To pluck from them their burden of little blue *Littorina* shells is to feel the skeletal remains of creatures born into a warmer Baltic Sea some 5,000 years ago.

Land upheaval has resulted in the need for special legislation to determine ownership of the new territory. Much use has been made by lawyers, in the solution of their disputes, of the legacy of old maps. The theme has been explored by Michael Jones who, taking his title from Zacharias Topelius, has presented his findings for English readers in his book *Finland, a Daughter of the Sea* (1977).

The boulder in Petalax, with its iron ring, stands as a symbol of the granite and also of the power of the ice to mould it — even to move it. In turn, granite — perhaps more precisely the family of pre-Cambrian rocks of which it is a member — stands as a symbol for Finland.

The variety of Finland's primeval rocks is to be seen most clearly around the edges of the land where they are exposed to sea and lake. In colour they may be grey, pink, mottled or coppery red. They may be veined with glittering quartz, patterned with toffee-coloured swirls, fractured by vulcanicity, scoured and scored by ice, washed smooth by waves, enamelled in the sunlight. There are crumbling of 'rotten' granites (*rapakivi*), which weather into granules. There are pock-marked granites, the chemical components of which result in their differential erosion. There are marvellously moulded granites along the littoral of the isles of Kökar, the mammelated shapes of which might have been a playground for the English sculptor Henry Moore. There are bold and billowing formations that look like the solidified waves of the sea itself. In Geta parish there are rocky caverns, such as Clod's stuga, bearing the names of mythological ancestors. In Kallskär there are water-worn kettle holes. Smooth cliff-faces are to be seen along the proto-fiords of Åland's north coast, at Astuvansalmi in Ristiina parish, where Stone Age hunters have chiselled their frescoes. In the Swedish-speaking archipelagos, a hard monosyllabic vocabulary has evolved to describe the rocky features *kobbe, kulle, klint, klippa, krok, klev, vik, skarv, nabb.*

Most of the granites have been slow to yield to manipulation by man. Medieval churches were constructed from available boulders and loose slabs. 'Speckled hen' churches, they were called, from the varied colour of the stones between the mortar. Fortresses and the substantial barns of the larger farms have a similar appearance. For a long time it was easier to make bricks than to quarry and carry stone, although the porphyry of Ruskeala was deemed worthy of quarrying for monumental use in St Petersburg. To walk across Senate Square in Helsinki is to appreciate the meaning of 'the stone city'. An army of stonemasons must have been needed to trim, shape and lay the granite setts, foundation blocks, flag-stones, kerbstones and flights of steps. And from where did the stalwart little Finnish horses transport it all in their wooden carts? And when did steam-powered splitting, dressing and polishing ease the working of granite?

It was natural that Finland should produce a master of granite — Lars Sonck. It almost seems as though he was playing with the litter of granite slabs and boulders bequeathed by the Ice Age. They give to Tampere cathedral its craggy mood: they are essential to Sibelius's villa Ainola. The parliament building in Helsinki gives an almost moral authority to granite — a Shakespearian 'sermon in stone'. The grey granite of Kuru is the more aesthetically pleasing when set beside the flights of Carrara marble steps in Tampere *talo*.

The coming of dynamite that has allowed the deepening of quarries has also enabled granite outcrops to be levelled and the endless twists and turns in highways and railways to be reduced. The cliffs of granite through which motorways have been blasted glow and glint in the setting sun. Towns echo to the thud and thump of explosions on building sites. Farmers are freed of the labour of removing obstructive boulders. New rock-drilling methods, devised in Finland, have transformed tunnelling. The Church-in-the-Rock in Helsinki was a relatively simple excavation: Helsinki's underground railways a more costly undertaking. The virtual Hall of the Mountain King at Retretti, near Savonlinna, is a prototype for new underground entertainment places. Man-made storage caves have become economically possible. Even more important is the greater ease with which tens of thousands of kilometres of underground channels for drainage, water supply, district heating and cabling can disregard obstructive granite. The pre-Cambrian era has yielded to late twentieth-century technology.

Landscape into words

Robert Louis Stevenson, in his essay on *Walking Tours*, sought to 'set the landscape to words'. One word which sums up the Finnish landscape is 'epigrammatic'. The essential features — rock, water, bog, woodland and the clearances made by man repeat themselves in an infinity of combinations. For the passenger who speeds through in car or train the result appears repetitious; but for the pedestrian the landscape changes perpetually and is pleasing in its variety. The reaction to it depends on the observer. The sharp-eyed Selina Bunbury, taking her *A Summer in Northern Europe* in 1856, wrote of plain John Bull dismissing the landscape as monotonous. For her, any-thing but plain Mrs John Bull, there was 'always some new shape, some curious appearance, some changing effect' to challenge such a reaction. The nineteenth-century Finnish artist Väinö Blomstedt had a contrasting reaction — 'Finland's nature can only confuse a man's head to the degree that he doesn't know how to grasp it.' Ultimately, in the Finnish landscape, it is the nuances that count.

For the longer-distance traveller the visually monotonous attribute derives from the general absence of dramatic relief over the greater part of the country. Again, except at or near the water's edge, the traveller is often sur-rounded by forest. It is a closed landscape, not an open one. Many roads run through walls of trees, above which rise spidery structures which are the look-out towers of fire watchers, bulbous water-towers and the occasional factory chimney with its plume of smoke.

From the outermost skerries, which look like schools of porpoises in the dancing waves, peninsular Finland rises through the low-lying shores of the twin gulfs of the Baltic to the bold ridges that constitute the watershed between the Eastsea, the White Sea and the Arctic Ocean. The worn-down surface of its bedrock supports a great litter of deposits. Some are of glacial origin; some are the product of the sea responding to uplift. Landwards, deposits derive from the shrinking lakes or the rivers as they cut down to the bedrock on their way to the sea. A great morainic arc, the Salpausselkä, sweeps around southern Finland from Karelia in the east to the Hangö area, losing itself in the coastal waters beyond Jurmo island. It is not especially impressive visually, except where man-made structures lift the observer above the tree-tops or where sand and gravel pits slash open the surface. Much more fascinating from the human point of view are the sinuous ridges that worm their way across the lakes, their narrow crests supporting historic routeways and their tree-clad flanks dropping to sandy beaches.

Finland has been described for generations as a land of lakes. It is less commonly recorded that there are at least as many islands. 'An island is the opposite of a lake,' runs the poem by W.H. Auden, who thought of Finland for a possible journey in 1938, but ended up in Iceland from where he wrote his celebrated letters. Individual Finnish lakes boast islands by the score. Koitere, in the east, in the words of the poet August Ahlqvist is a 'hundred-island lake'. Individual constituents of the richly-ramified Saimaa lake system may claim as many islands as there are days in the year. Seascapes and lakescapes look much the same, with frequently similar aquatic plants fringing their shores and linking their islands. Water buttercups forget that they are in the sea. So do the reed meadows of *Phragmites*. Seaweeds lose their vigour towards the near freshwater heads of the Gulf of Bothnia and the Gulf of Finland.

As rivers go, the waterways that drain the lakes are youthful in years. They are generally shallow and are strewn with the rapids that they create as they cut into the bedrock. The northern rivers have their fair share of waterfalls, with the turbulent Kitkajoki and Oulankajoki draining to the White Sea through ancient gorges: with Arctic Lake Inari a great reservoir for Paatsjoki, the boundary river that flows between Norway and Russia to the Barents Sea. The Vuoksi and Kymi rivers break through the Salpausselkä barrier in torrent courses which have cheered hydro-electric engineers. The Vuoksi channel and the Imatra rapids were among the first Finnish tourist attractions, while the rapids near the estuary of the Kymi river claimed the attention of Alexander III of Russia, who built a fishing lodge near the then salmon-rich river. The rivers of Ostrobothnia, sometimes breaking through a dune-lined coast, retain the reputation as salmon rivers that they had already acquired over four centuries ago when Olaus Magnus included woodcuts of both the fish and their predators, the seals, on his pictorial map *Carta marina*.

Between the land and water are the swamps or boglands, in human terms the least pleasant of the natural landscapes. They claim the first sentence of Väinö Linna's classic novel *Here under the North Star* — 'In the beginning was the swamp, the mattock — and Jussi.' The Finnish environmentalist Reino Kalliola once described Finland's swamps as being like 'innumerable variations on a melancholy melody' — the metaphor perhaps underscored by the insectivorous orchestra of the summer season. About a third of the country supports swamps, mires or bogs, with so-called blanket bog widespread in Lapland. The Finns have conceived their own terminology for them, and Finland claims a greater diversity of mire vegetation than any area of equal size. There has been much reclamation of swampland, sometimes of quite extensive areas by individual farmers — 'Swamp Czars' in Linna's terminology. Liminka in northern Ostrobothnia is recalled, where the shallow peatlands are now covered by extensive grasslands, and support numberless hay barns — *latomeri*, in the local dialect, a veritable sea of sheds. Elsewhere, afforestation of reclaimed bogland is widespread.

Woodland remains the dominant element of the Finnish scene. It frames the landscape over four-fifths of the country — the pine prevailing on the drier lands and defining the limits of coniferous occurrence both altitudinally and latitudinally. Northwards, it is often accompanied by a grey cover of lichen, popularly called reindeer moss. The spruce dominates on moister soils. The birch lightens and brightens the dark green of the conifers — 'so much dark forest', laments Bo Carpelan's *Axel*. In a contorted and shrubby form the birch presses on beyond the frontiers of the pine in the north, ultimately assuming a creeping, dwarf-like character, the mouse-ear birch, in the tundra. Scattered areas of primeval forest (*urskog*) remain, shaggy and unkempt, having escaped fire and the hand of man.

There are residual oak groves in the extreme south-west. Coupled with stands of hazel along the coastal margins of Åland and Åboland, they provide the background to the *lövängar* — the deciduous meadowlands which Carl Linnaeus called the parklands of the peasantry. In such places as Idö and Brunskär, they provide botanical climaxes which support several hundreds of plant species. Beyond such Botany Bays, where pharmacopoeia of medicinal plants may be found, lie the rocky skerries. They are the areas of primary plant colonisation, with airborne, waterborne and bird-borne seeds producing a profusion of vegetation in the pockets of sea dung that accumulate in the rocky interstices. In the skerries, nature matches the skills of the Japanese gardener as well as offering a paradise for the lichenographer.

Between the rocks and the water and out of the forests and the swamplands, the Finns have established the places where they live and work. They have transformed the sterile places as well as occupying the fertile. Arable land is still seamed with the original open ditches in many places. There are natural meadowlands, which are often flooded in spring: there are patches of grazing land (*hagmark*) marginal to the woodlands and spry with junipers. Although continuous with Russia, Norway and Sweden, the Finnish imprint on the land is subtly different.

Because population density is low, the absolute impact of man upon wildlife has been more limited than in many European countries. The decline in the number of marauding animals — wolf and lynx in winter and bear in summer (only partly satisfying his appetite with ten kilos of berries a day) — has favoured the multiplication of browsing animals. Immense numbers of elk damage the woodlands and trespass on the farmlands. There are licences to kill 70,000 annually. Wild reindeer occur as well as domesticated herds. The squirrel has taken to urban life with gusto. The seal, preying on salmon and *siika*, is the enemy of the fisherman.

Woods and waters are alive with summer birds, gamebirds, waterfowl, waders. The sea-eagle puts in an appearance — even the eagle.

The round of the year

Landscape is inseparable from climate, for it changes visually with the swing of the seasons. The visitor to Finland is always conscious of high latitude, with its accompanying rhythm of daylight and darkness, warmth and cold. Finland has been called a land of three winters — autumn winter, high winter and spring winter. Even after radiant March suns, April's *takatalvi* (winter's back end) can be dispiriting, with its snow-smeared countryside, its dissolving winter ice and brown floodwaters. Spring is 'lazy', as Xavier Marmier put it, 'turning a deaf ear to human entreaties'. There can also be a touch of winter in summer to the extent that in some years summer may be 'green winter' over a third of the land. The threat of summer frosts, *halla*, was an early spur to agricultural insurance. In such a setting, midsummer and midwinter solstices are more significant than equinoxes. 'I vote for spring, autumn gets in, winter forms the cabinet,' opines the poet Paavo Haavikko. Winter is the stern saga, summer a fleeting legend. There is excusable indulgence in summer's precious opportunities simply because of the dominance of winter. In summer, Finland returns to its rural or maritime roots. There is a search for sanctuaries: often for isolation. The convectional thunder storms of July (especially notorious in the so-called 'women's week', when all 'name days' in the almanach are feminine) may disturb the *al fresco* life. The flicker of summer lightning (*elosalama*) reminds Finns of their continental setting. So does the hot wind that sometimes blows from Russia, especially late in the season. Autumn, draining the countryside of colour, is rarely the season of 'mists and mellow fruitfulness' of Western Europe, but it is 'the season of synthesis' for the poet Elmer Diktonius.

Naturally the winter circumstance is simply accepted by those who are brought up in its rigorous régime. In former times, everybody and everything took cover, the stove became the centre of life, conservation of calories was critical. Work rhythms changed. The water-driven sawmill might be out of action for weeks on end; axe men and sawmen went into the forests; ice-saws came out; ice-cellars were filled. There were compensations. The runner replaced the wheel. Direct routes across frozen water replaced tortuous summer tracks: smooth sleigh passages, the rough routes of carriage ways. Winter was the season for making up accounts according to Zachris Topelius's merchant. It was also the time when there was at least a measure of sociability. Summer in bygone days was a hard season in many ways. So much work had to be crammed into such a short time in the near-merciless summer daylight. Frans Eemil Sillanpää has captured the mood of summer resignation, of the 'weariness of unremitting hours' spent in the fields.

The impact of winter has always been exaggerated by outsiders. Sir John Norris, writing to the Admiralty in London on September 11, 1720, towards the end of the Great Northern War, imparted that 'The bad season does now come on so fast that the end of the month is the longest time we would venture to be in these parts.' Even assuming the climate to have been colder than today, the threat of the Baltic freezing over could scarcely have been so great. It was the same in the autumn of 1854 at the time of the Crimean War. Could British men-of-war really have been draped with icicles in October, as depicted in the *Illustrated London News*?

Half a century of technological development, with every new facility taken for granted, has produced a total change in the attitude to winter. Given more than sufficient calories, it is necessary to dispose of the surplus in winter exercise. A century ago, the *concours d'élégance* was the ambition of all who skated, while the ski, though growing in popularity, had yet to make its mark. Today, almost half of Finland's population must have proficiency certificates in skiing. Simultaneously, great new marathons have taken their place in sporting calendars — ski marathons, skating marathons — attracting thousands, and all independent of the great climax of ski-jumping at Lahti. There is an aesthetic sensitivity to ice and snow, with photographers seeking examples of the winter art of the wind. Apart from the broken bones and twisted tendons resulting from falls on the ice, winter is a healthier season of the year than in more southern climes. 'Elle fortifie et endurcit les corps: elle nous délivre d'une infinité de maladies,' wrote an anonymous author to the old *Finska Hushållningssällskapet*.

The beauty and colour of winter in Finland were first extolled by Zacharias Topelius over a century ago. Since then, no one has used words more effectively to describe the Finnish winter than the French writer Georges Duhamel in his essay *Chant du Nord* (1931). No one has caught the winter scene on film more attractively than Christopher Irons, whose reels it is to be hoped have been stored somewhere for posterity. It has been fascinating to see how formerly soberly clothed winter — grey, black, brown, dark blue — has taken upon itself a profusion of colours. And they are colours which are the antithesis of nature, the winter wear of ermine, hare and woodcock. From top to toe, clothing has become defiantly colourful. Ski-wear, skis and all their accessories seem brighter still in sunny spring-winter. Even fur coats, even when for social reasons they are not worn inside-out, may suffer tinting. A lilac-coloured fox must be the nadir. In fact, furs which were traditionally worn for protection against the cold, have been largely replaced by equally efficient man-made fibres.

Winter calls for heavy expenditure on lighting and heating. Darkness has been challenged by floodlighting and the rainbow colouring of extravagantly employed neon-strip lighting. At the domestic level, the *per capita* consumption of candles must approach a world record. There are candles for cosiness and for commemoration. There are candles in public as well as private windows on December 6, in Borgå's windows on Runeberg's birthday, in churchyards and cemeteries on Christmas Eve.

Heat has to be generated somewhere and has to be paid for, although conversely Finland is relieved of the costs of summer air-conditioning. Engineers have invented the concept of thermal space when estimating heating costs (how, one is prompted to ask, does it correlate with the liquid space of *avantgarde* architects?).

There is inevitably heavy expenditure on keeping open lines of communication — roads and runways, railways and shipping lanes. The frequency of hard winters may have diminished in recent decades, but the need for icebreakers and ice-strengthened shipping has to be constantly reviewed, not least in the light of insurance costs. The Baltic Sea — *mare glacialis, mare tenebrosum*, throughout many winters till the end of the nineteenth century — is now beamed upon by the floodlights of immense ferries that grind through the ice. Within two generations, ice-forecasting systems have reached a peak of sophistication — a far cry from the *Ice Atlas* that Finnish scientists pioneered in 1937.

It was a casual comment by Hillar Kallas, then of the Finnish section of the B.B.C., that set firmly in motion a study of *Winter in Finland* and an eventual joint publication with Helmer Smeds. The subject opened up a whole variety of topics. One sprang out of the logbooks of the icebreaker fleet, stored in the archive of the Maritime Research Institute and made available by its welcoming staff. Another led to the street cleansing department of the city of Helsinki and the ways in which its officials handled ice and snow. An unexpected luncheon invitation was received. The executives of an oil company were interested in the operation by Finns of a compressed-air system with underwater distributors for keeping open shipping channels in winter (Atlas Copco was already operating a similar system on Lake Mälaren). The chain of enquiries that this started led in many directions. Horlicks, the malted milk company in Slough, England, had taken out a patent for a similar system. By way of Ilmari Hustich, then Minister of Trade, it was discovered that Enso-Gutzeit had invented an independent system for keeping open log basins on Lake Saimaa during winter. The process was then discovered to have been conceived as one of the secret weapons for use against Russian tanks as they crossed the ice during the later war years. In fact, nearly half a century earlier, Canadians had used a compressed air system for keeping open a channel on the old St Lawrence Canal.

The upshot of the winter challenge has been that Finland has emerged as a specialist in 'cold design', from building and construction, through engineering devices and mechanical gadgetry to clothing. It has established its own Arctic Research Centre at the University of Lapland in Rovaniemi.

One foot in the sea

Finland has one foot in the sea, from which the land is rising, albeit unevenly. The Baltic is not one of the world's seven seas, but it has its own characteristics. It is a virtual inland sea, shallow with sluggish currents. It has low salinity and is almost brackish at the heads of the Gulfs of Bothnia and Finland. The tidal influence is weak, although the sea-level rises and falls significantly in response to barometric pressure. Storm-force winds are especially significant after winter high-pressure systems have induced the icing of extensive areas of water. They can pile up great reefs of pack ice.

Water temperatures respond quickly to short-term climatic changes; so, too, does marine life. Cod, for example, are especially sensitive to a fall in temperature. The virtually enclosed basin also exaggerates the effects of pollution on marine life — from the penny-sized dabs and half-penny sized jelly fish to seals.

Between its twin gulfs, the peninsula of Finland — Suomenniemi — points to the sea, the route to the outside world. 'Nature invites us to the sea,' wrote Augustin Ehrensvärd. And to the sea they go — some 7,000 seamen, in a fleet of ships on average no more than seven years old and totalling some two million tons. The most maritime province is Åland, an archipelago of countless islands. Symbolic of its relation to the sea is the sculpture which stands above Mariehamn's west harbour and bears the inscription 'Vår väg är havet'.* The saga of Åland's marriage with the sea is told in its maritime museum. The living testimony of the old Cape Horners, who sailed the province's fleet of clipper ships, is dying out, but there are plenty of words on paper and a fair number on tape. *The Last Grain Race* by Eric Newby remains a classic; so, too, is Pamela Eriksson's *The Duchess* (both books recall a summer evening in 1956 when, under the watchful eye of the Commodore, Eric Newby and Pamela Eriksson's daughter scaled the sooty rigging of the *Cutty Sark* at Greenwich). Words as well as deeds stick in the mind. 'It was like the second day of creation for weeks on end,' commented a sailor who had responded to the siren song of the sea and found himself in the Roaring Forties. Equally personal are the maritime experiences woven into the plots of her novels by Anni Blomqvist, whose stories are set amid the storm-tossed seas that batter the homes of Ålandic fisherfolk. Fiction can be turned to fact. There are recollections of a memorial service for Anni's husband and son. A flotilla of

*The sea is our highway.

open-decked motor boats, fishing boats and leisure craft were lashed together at the presumed place off Björkö where the fishermen were lost. Choirs sang, prayers were offered, wreaths were cast on the waves — and then the entire ceremony came abruptly to an end as the waters began to heave. *Havet giver: havet tar.**

The Ålandic experience is many-sided. Manifold legends of smuggling have been told — from the period of prohibition, the war years and the lean times that followed the war. A high-powered coastguard fleet keeps watch today. To have experienced their skilled manoeuvring on university trips to the outermost skerries is to realise their potential for bringing swift retribution to lawbreakers.

Finland is a land of many ships. They first multiplied in the nineteenth-century heyday of the sailing vessel. Every small port seems to have a record of shipyards where schooners, barques and brigs were built for the increasingly lively carrying trade. The primitive cameras of the day took photographs of carpenters, caulkers and handymen working on Noah's Ark-like vessels, propped in their slipways before launching. It was the period when shipping was mostly owned and operated collectively by the farming kith and kin of the captain. Turn the pages of *Åbo Underrättelser* from the time and reference may be found to as many as thirty-two people sharing in the ownership of a vessel of several hundred tons. 'A coffee pot and a share in a trading vessel are reckoned among the necessities of life,' runs a letter from 1875. It was largely a seasonal trade, with ships hauled ashore before the winter freeze, although some moved to the Mediterranean and others risked the high seas in search of more lucrative trade. Yellowing and often well-thumbed log books, telling tales of adventurous voyages, have been gathered into the archive of Åbo's maritime museum, with its accompanying minor treasury of nautical instruments. Iron and steam put an end to the age of wood. Nevertheless some of the early ships live on, cossetted as leisure vessels and speeded with auxiliary motor engines.

Shipbuilding remains important for Finland, but it is an industry sensitive to international trading fluctuations. Since the end of the Second World War, Finland has made a remarkable contribution to the world's mercantile marine. Much of its shipping had been lost in the war and such vessels of consequence as remained, including all of its modest icebreaker fleet, were surrendered to the U.S.S.R. as part of the war reparations. It was a matter of starting from scratch. Several ancient ferries bearing nostalgic names — *Wellamo*, *Oihonna*, *Bore* — kept the route to Stockholm alive with the aid in winter of Swedish icebreakers. Accordingly, shipyards were the object of immediate attention. The old Crichton

*The sea gives, the sea takes away.

Vulcan yards in Turku, recalling the name of an eighteenth-century immigrant ship's architect, sprang to life. A new name was heard in Helsinki — Wärtsilä.

It was exciting to witness the emergence of the impressive shipyards at Hietalahti. They were responsible for the construction of a fleet of icebreakers that was to overcome the challenge of the winter freeze. National success brought international attention. By the end of the 1950s Sweden and the U.S.S.R. were vying with Finland itself for bigger and better models. Most of the Arctic icebreaker fleet of the U.S.S.R. was constructed in Finnish yards. By the 1970s, Finland had become the world's leading producer of icebreakers and, with its elaborate research and model-testing facilities, an authority on ice-strengthened shipping. Little by little, its struggle with winter shipping has been eased and increasingly there is access to the innermost ports of the twin gulfs. Indeed, financial costs apart, there is no reason why all of Finland's ports should not be kept open throughout the year except in the most exceptional winters. In severe winters, skilled crews, women as well as men, may be engaged in intensive activity for several weeks on end, their accommodation high above the powerful machinery which enables icebreakers to ride upon, rock upon and eventually collapse resistant pack ice. Ice need only imprison Finland when highly unionised labour chooses to bring icebreaker services to a halt.

Given yards with a capacity to build large-scale icebreakers, it became possible for Finland to tender for other types of vessel in the international market. The demand for cruise liners provided substantial orders for shipyards at Helsinki, Turku and Rauma. A fleet of liners commissioned by Norwegian shipping companies for Caribbean waters was followed by successful tendering for the 40,000-ton *Royal Princess* in the mid-1980s. In total contrast were the floating dormitories built for Soviet construction workers engaged on projects along Russia's internal waterways. An eye was also kept on the international market for oil rigs and platforms, cable layers and conversions and repairs.

Domestically, the production of ferries has helped declining order-books. Finland's Baltic ferries, computer-built and largely computer-operated, with their arcades of shops and restaurants, are unrivalled in their facilities and efficiency.

Sea Finland was an appropriate title for a memorable exhibition mounted by the Finns at the National Maritime Museum, Greenwich, in 1987 and visited by an immense flood of summer tourists. The more fortunate of them were able to board the formidable icebreaker *Sampo*, dressed overall and in holiday mood on the June waters of the Thames. Who could have forecast that within a year or two tour operators would be calling into service unemployed units of the icebreaker fleet to provide holiday-makers with a new winter experience? And who, on seeing the pioneering diving suit invented by a Finn in the eighteenth century, could have anticipated that two centuries later, summer tourists would be seeing the sub-aquatic sights of Lake Inari through the portholes of a Finnish-built leisure submarine?

The response to the land

There is an undeniable but scientifically inexplicable consonance between people and the land they live in. 'Our land is of us and we are of the land,' was the simple conclusion of Topelius, writing at a time before geographical determinism had wide currency as a theory. Rock, soil, water, forest — all enter into the relationship. West Europeans speak of their 'grassroots': perhaps 'forest roots' are more appropriate for Finns. *Metsässä syntynyt metsässä kasvanut.** Frans Michael Franzén described himself as 'a child of our rocks'. Even more than Henry Adam's New Englanders, Finns are 'sons of granite and of ice'. L. Dudley Stamp wrote of 'the amphibious Finn', echoing a phrase of Sir Thomas Browne that 'man is an amphibious piece'. The ungenerous, leached soils, which many pioneers have reclaimed — and on which many Finns found themselves when they emigrated to the upper states of the American Mid-West — have tempted one author to call Finns 'podsol men'.

At the local level, it is natural that the names on the map should spring out of the land and those on the hydrographic chart out of the water. More intimately, the features of land and water have yielded farm names: farm names, family names. To the foreigner all Finnish names look alien, but a dictionary soon shows them to consist of the old familiar components of other tongues. Sometimes a name is untranslatable; sometimes a geographical feature. Such names inevitably imply a feature which, if not unique to Finland, is a phenomenon that it only shares with neighbouring territories. Ecologically speaking, there are common features all the way to the White Sea coast.

The months of the year, neither classical nor mythological, have also sprung mostly out of the natural world: *helmikuu* (the pearly grey month of February), *maaliskuu* (the month of rising sap), *huhtikuu* (the month for clearing the woodlands), *heinäkuu* (the haymaking month), *kesäkuu* (the month of summer) through to *marraskuu* (November, the month of death). There are inevitable regional variations in the response to the land. Natural provinces have their own identities, although administrative units more appropriate to contemporary linkages have replaced them. The historic provinces of Uusimaa (Nyland), Häme (Tavastland), Savo (Savolax), Kainuu, Karelia and Lappi (Lapland) remain realities at the human level.

*Born in the forest: reared in the forest.

Their distinctive characteristics have been sought out by ethnographers. Many migrants retain their regional dialects, religious attitudes and customs after they have left their native provinces. Regional patriotism generates regional rivalries — even regional pecking orders. 'It isn't a crime to be born in Savo,' say the Ostrobothnians, 'but it's a pity.' And again, 'When someone born in Savo speaks, the listener is responsible for what he hears.' Theoretically, with the new technical integration of Finland, it might be assumed that the traditional units would tend to coalesce in the greater whole. It is not necessarily so.

There are landscape gradations from north to south and from west to east. Much of the high north is wilderness. In fact, one and a half million hectares of Lapland have been protected by the Wilderness Act of 1991. Lapland has its own character and induces its own reactions. The Lappologist Samuli Paulaharju wrote of it as being 'verily from the great hand of God and a marvellous work of creation'. Others have found it less appealing — 'melancholy in its enormity'. Four habitats have been ascribed to the province — *tunturi*-Lappi (the Lapland of the open fells), *metsä*-Lappi (the thinly wooded Lapland with bearded pines), *outa*-Lappi and *aapa*-Lappi (the Lapland of tussocked swamps and dark rivers). Only a part of the administrative province of Lapland is occupied by Lapps or *Same*. Kalevi Rikkinen has made the happy suggestion that the northern quarter of Lappi might be renamed *Saamemaa* (the Land of *Same*).

In total contrast to the high north is Finland's deep south. The extensive use of land in the north contrasts with its intensive employment in the south. In general, the landscapes of the south are the most humanised in Finland. They are pleasantly domesticated, neat and tidy though not so manicured as those of Denmark. They offer what Aleksis Kivi called 'a friendly mother face'. Occasionally, a touch of extravagance enters the scene. In the parks of several scores of entailed estates, and inspired in varying degrees by the models of Western Europe, native trees have been replaced by exotic 'noble' trees — oak, chestnut, beech, silver willow — which struggle to survive on the frontiers of their cultivation. Here and there, the minor paradises of artists have survived. They are to be found in lakeside Tuusula, with Pekka Halonen's atelier, Eero Järnefelt's villa, Syväranta manor behind its spider's web gates. But art is outshone by nature in the south-western archipelagos. Here, the island world has a threefold identity — inner *skärgård*, middle *skärgård* and outer *skärgård*. It has been exciting to witness success crowning the struggle to protect the seascapes of Åbo archipelago with the creation of the Archipelago national park.

The speed with which national parks and conservation areas have multiplied during the last generation is evident from the *Atlas of Finland*. In the 1960 edition, neither claimed space: in the current edition, they fill an entire section. Such protected landscapes were described by the American Walter Stegner as 'a part of the geography of hope'. Their aesthetic as well as their scientific appreciation in late twentieth-century Finland is another measure of the advance from a land of promise to a promised land.

3

CHAMBERS OF CONSCIOUSNESS

'Whatever captivates the eye or intoxicates the ears, charms
the taste, makes delicious the nostrils with its smell, caresses
the sense of touch was contained within that place of places.'
(Alan of Lille, *Anticlaudianus*, 1183)

A sharpening of the senses

At the end of the eighteenth century, Finland enjoyed a school of natural
scientists who were inspired by Linnaeus to follow the principles of his
Instructio peregrenatoris. They were assiduous collectors and classifiers,
empiricists who sought to sharpen their faculty of observation that they
might unravel some of the secrets of nature. Henrik Gabriel Porthan
encouraged them in their endeavours. He believed that in the process their
'feelings [would] be refined'. He was also of the opinion that it was all the
senses in combination that helped to fix a land and its people in the mind.
Maailma on minun aistieni runoelma. 'The world is a poem of my senses,'
wrote Eeva-Liisa Manner.

When he sought to capture the image of a landscape, the Finnish
geographer J.G. Granö averred: 'We are bound to our sensations, even
though we may place all manner of instruments that magnify or specify
between our research object and our senses.' And all those 'airborne
particles' that the senses catch and store in the chambers of consciousness
create at particular times and in particular places what the French essayist
Amiel described as *un état de l'âme*.

Accordingly, no excuse is offered for a celebration in the context of
Finland of 'the five wisdoms of the soul', as William Blake called them.
Perhaps there might be added to sight, smell, sound, touch and taste a sixth
sense, for that too belongs to the personal experience of Finland.

Paysage sonore

Every country has its particular combinations of sound: the sounds of
nature and the sounds of man. They constitute an acoustic world, a
soundscape, a *paysage sonore*.

The sea has its sounds. The ceaseless roar of storm waves breaking on
the perilous shores of northern Åland can be mentally exhausting. Only a
battery of timpani and kettle drums could reproduce the noise of ice floes
breaking about the hulls of winter shipping. There are memories of the
whisperings of summer breezes blowing through the reed-beds that line

shallow seashores, of the menacing rustle of late August winds in Eckerö's withered midsummer poles, the sound of autumn gales in forests around Nurmes. The blizzard may moan, but eventually snow muffles sound. The sifting of dry snow through leafless vegetation is matched by the thin wind that seeks a passage through the gummed paper that seals old window-frames. It recalls the sound that children make blowing through paper wrapped round combs . . . Spring winter offers the slither of roof-top snow, the grinding of ice floes on melting rivers, the gurgle and spit of drainpipes.

There are workaday sounds — the circular saw whining in numberless mills, the chain-saw and axe doing battle in the woodland, the whirring sound (like the flight of a disturbed partridge) addressed by the forester to his horse. There are muffled explosions that signify yet another assault on obstructive bedrock on building sites. Along the waterfront, the *basso profundo* chug of the working motor-boat answers the impolite roar of the speedboat: the deep sirens of seagoing vessels contrast with the echoing hooters of lakeland steamers. The perky toot of the grandfatherly genera-tion of railway engines is not yet obsolete, though the contented chuffing of wood-burning steam engines sitting idly in railway sidings is but a memory. Braking automobiles squeal on the granite setts of city streets. In Helsinki the trams emit a *glissando* hum sufficiently attractive in its modulations to provide motifs for a musical composition.

The quiet rubbing and scrubbing by the water's edge of rag rugs con-trasts with the dawn or dusk ceremony of carpet-beating from urban balconies or in echoing backyards (is it a housewifely therapy incapable of replacement by the vacuum cleaner?). Still, in some homes, the loom rattles and the spinning wheel vibrates softly. And, always, there is the hissing, spitting and cracking of the sauna stones.

There are bird songs. A displaced Karelian farmer friend finds time to write lyrically about them in his work diary. The whooper swan — *laulujoutsen*, surely the Swan of Tuonela — thrives again. There are memories of the cry of an occasional crane, of a solitary corncrake in summer twilight at Frugård (recalling Eino Leino's *Nocturne*), of the croaking ravens around Turku cathedral, of the curiously plaintive lament of autumn finches, of the ubiquitous gull cry and the quack of ducks in alarmed flight. Nightingales at Svartå in June stir recollections of eight-eenth-century Åbo romanticism, especially of Jacob Bonsdorff's apotheosis of summer — a boat on Borgå river with a flute echoing between the rocks and stirring bird song.

Doubtless, wolves howl though few hear them any more. All are con-scious of the noises made by many small creatures — the scuttle and squeak of squirrels, the hum of bees, the electric chatter of high-summer grasshoppers, the ominous whine of mosquitos.

Above and below these sounds of nature, there are bells — the mournful bells of bobbing buoys, the off-key ting-tang of bells at level crossings, cow bells, sheep bells, sleigh bells. There is the ding-dong of Lutheran church bells:

> *O at mit ljud dig rörde så*
> *Att du till kyrkan ville gå.**

— as engraved on Hammarland bell in 1765. On Saturday evenings, there are the more clamorous Orthodox bells. In Helsinki, the angelus booms across Senate Square. Why was the incongruous bell that used to reverberate around the central well of Stockmann's store installed? Why was it silenced?

There are the sounds of music. Some cannot be recaptured — Sibelius's 'endless concerts for birds' performed on a rock at Vanajavesi and his fantasies for the sea played on a skerry shore (vignettes gleaned from Erik Tawaststjerna's incomparable biography). Happily, the richest of musical tapestries has been woven on disc and tape since the master's passing. Numberless Finnish choirs make music — earnestly. The military band parades down the Esplanade on its way to the presidential palace, not quite in tune. The sound of the accordion, often crafted in Lahti, is never far away. It is less the monopoly of the sailor than formerly; even the schoolroom has taken it over. Joined to the fiddle, it sets folk-dancers twirling. There are the faint vibrations of the wind-harp: the soft hootings of the birch-bark lur. Above all, there is the distinctive *kantele*. Earliest recollections are of an English hymn-tune in a Madetoja setting played by Erkki Kurki-Suonio in Iisalmi. There is the familiar interval tune on Kuopio radio, plucking out the opening bars of the *Kallavesi* folksong. There are happy memories of the valiant efforts of junior schoolchildren to master the strings of their national instrument.

Finland is not without bizarre musical sounds — Lapp joiking and the throaty chromatic wail of the dying breed of professional weeping women. Both are a civilisation away from the festivals of chamber music in Kuhmo or jazz in Pori.

The sound of language itself is of the essence of Finland. John Scott Keltie, writing in the eleventh edition of the *Encyclopaedia Britannica*, proclaimed Finnish to be 'the most sonorous and harmonious of tongues'. Aurélien Sauvageot put into words the characteristic sounds of the Finnish language with a fluency and precision that only a French scholar could achieve — '*un peu rauque et saccadé . . . Les voyelles marquent: elles éclatent joyeusement sur les lèvres*'. The reverberatory 'r' is trilled out

---

*O that my sound would stir you so/That to the church door you would go.

by Finns even more effectively than by the Scots. For some Europeans, wrote a Finnish historian, the Finnish language sounded as incomprehensible as 'the twittering of birds'. Dialect variations — *Savon murre*, for example, or *Rauman kieli* — only serve to confirm among foreigners the uniqueness of the Finnish language. *Finlands svensk*, 'not a dialect but a language of its own', has more familiar sounds.

Pleasure can be brought to the alien ear by the sound of Finnish words, simple monosyllabic ones such as are poetically enshrined in the verse of Uuno Kailas. Place-names can charm — Merimasku, Meriluoto, Orimattila, Orivesi. Patrick Leigh-Fermor could profitably repeat for Finland his essay on Greek place-names and the spells that they cast even in their printed form. Take a parish — Kuhmo. Choose at random half-a-dozen names — Sivakka, Riihivaara, Kamarakylä, Ypykkävaara, Hauhilonkylä, Kiekikoski — and the effect can be the same.

'The aesthetic of silence', as Susan Sontag puts it, can also be appreciated in Finland. Silence is to be found among the craggy *vaarat* of north-east Kainuu and among the austere *tunturit* of Lapland where, in the words of Edith Södergran, 'The sun is king and the queen is silence.' Indeed, in winter much of Finland is smothered in Jack London's 'white silence'. In summer, Georges Duhamel experienced what he called Finland's veritable 'national parks of silence'. . . . Finns also know how to command silence. Public opinion prevented piped music being broadcast over the public address system on the trains and demanded its elimination from Helsinki's Academic Bookshop.

'The thinking eye'

Just as there are ears that do not hear, so there are eyes that do not see and eyes that only see. Paul Klee emphasised the importance of 'the thinking eye'. There is always something new to ponder in what is seen. For this reason Pekka Suhonen has captured the hitherto disregarded wind-etched pictures on the ice. There are visions to be seen in the darkness of winter, in the chiaroscuro created by moonlight. *Kaamosaika* provides new experiences, when daylight is reduced to a brief twilight and when the shifting curtains of the *aurora borealis* add a ghostly luminosity to the night scene. There can be velvety dark late summer nights. There is a memory of a pitch black night beside a Kustavi fairway, with every star in the firmament reflected back from the motionless waters, and another of the Pellinge archipelago when the full moon created a stairway of light across the ripples of the sea. A third memory is of a half-moon and all the stars caught in the luminous rigging of the *Pommern*, the whole framed in a bedroom window on the Mariehamn waterfront. For 'bedroom window' read 'magic casement'.

Finland can also be a shadow land. In fact, Rabbe Enckell has written of
it as a land of double shadows. A man's shadow can be many times longer
than himself as he stands on the smooth white surface of a frozen lake with
the setting sun behind him. Contrastingly, in wan November even the
shadows disappear and grey becomes the dominant colour. There are
leaden lakes with roundels of pale grey ice and ashen ploughland edged by
withered vegetation.

Winter's magpie land is, in fact, shot through with a spectrum of
colour. There are faint rainbows in the exhalations of sea smoke above
freezing coastal waters. There are rainbows in the ice itself, as Topelius
was anxious to point out to artists who thought that winter was colour-
less. There were rainbows for Edward Clarke in the curtains of icicles
hanging from the ice caves created by winter storms around the coast of
Åland. The not unusual green skies of frozen February above the golden
rim of the horizon may presage a hard frost, but they offer a fine display of
colour. For the poet Aaro Hellaakoski there was 'negative fire' in the
steely blue skies of winter.

At midsummer, flamboyant sunsets can be transformed into flamboyant
sunrises — Saariselkä supplies the memory. The midsummer bonfire, the
kokko, with its tongues of flame, competes with the orange dawn. The
first experience was at Nastola — a veritable ring of bonfires round the
lake. In the eyes of Valdemar Nyman, one-time vicar of Finström, the
setting sun can transform the granite, felspar, sandstones and quartz of
medieval church walls into jasper, onyx, carbuncle and lapis lazuli.
Finström church also has a florid relic in the crimson and gold of an
Orthodox priest's robe that found its way there through the medium of
President Franklin Roosevelt and a Finnish sailor. It is one with the
gleaming relics of the Orthodox Museum in Kuopio and the cloth-of-
gold canonicals remembered from a candle-lit service in Joensuu. Contrastingly, there are memories of early morning mists off Björkö when it
was possible to share the vision of the French traveller Léouzon le
Duc when he saw the Finnish sun as 'une lampe enfermée dans un globe
d'opal'.

There is a brief climax also above the tree-line in the tundra of Lapland
during ruska, the russet or red time at the onset of autumn. Beyond the
orange and lemon of the contorted birch scrub and the carmine of the
leaves of the fireweed, the creeping ground flora spread carpets of turkey-
red, burnt sienna, copper, even purple. Anthony Trollope wrote of 'the
accident of colour' fixing a landscape in the mind's eye. The landscape of
subarctic Kevo is fixed in the mind's eye through a September sunset
with the roadside vegetation ablaze with colour, its lantern-glow slow to
disappear.

The south knows more pastel shades. The anemone, blue or faintly pink,

announces the coming of spring. High summer in the archipelagos con-
jures up a flora of immense variety. At the edge of the sea, it is inseparable
from the quality of the light, which has an added brightness from the
reflections of the sun in the water. It is the season when islands take to the
air — mirages of woodland above the white-streaked sea. Skies can be
radiantly blue and white — cumulus piled high and too much like a
picture-postcard to be true. The dark blue swallow returns and the bottle-
green dragon-fly catches the eye with the tremor of its wings. . . . As
soon as autumn mists take over, the ground is covered with the gauze of a
myriad spiders' webs. At Tvärminne, arachnologists have identified more
than 1,000 different species. Fur farms have their own pastel shades — the
shining mink have become pearl, topaz and sapphire in hue.

An olfactory calculus

All nations probably have distinctive smells, reflects Jörn Donner. The
smell of Finland is essentially the smell of the forest. It is possible to smell
Finland before seeing it. On hot, hazy summer days, the resinous smell of
conifers drifts far out into the Baltic. So, too, does the smell of forest
fires — heavy on the air of a hot east wind blowing across the Russian
border. And, from the national to the local, there is a curious memory of
the oily smell lurking in the stains left on the wall of a boatshed from seal
skins nailed there as they were cured following a springtime shoot off
Replot.

Once upon a time, tar, pitch and charcoal burneries added their
olfactory contributions. Deal boards, seasoning in the yards of other lands,
yield a haunting smell of Finland. So, too, do the objects made from
juniper wood. Scents from the past are especially recalled when a hot sun
releases odours of tar-impregnated timbers from old buildings. It is a smell
redolent of open-air museums. It is also among the constituents that
combine to produce the unique smell of antediluvian saunas — a 'honey-
sweet' smell for Ilmarinen in Kalevala days. It is not only the body that is
cleansed by the löyly or vapour rising from the stones: the nostrils benefit
equally (both are more than cleansed if alcohol is also cast on the stones). A
special keenness in the sense of smell follows escape from the heat of the
sauna.

The birch in spring is a brief rival to the conifer. The scent of birch-
leaves on the cold night air following a warm day can be mildly intoxicating. The fragrance is even more evident when born on an easterly wind
from the thousands of square kilometres of birch woods in neighbouring
Russia. In winter, the dried birch whisk, flailed in the sauna, revives the
scent of summer.

In the countryside, wood smoke is always on the air, but the smoke derived from the cartloads of logs that were once thrust into urban basements to stoke winter stoves, belongs to the past. At the same time, diesel odours have replaced those of wood smoke and steam which formerly enveloped railway yards. Sometimes, in Ostrobothnia, peat smoke replaces wood smoke, though today the turbaries are used less for domestic purposes than for the generation of electricity.

Timber processing has its own calculus of smells. The radius of the scent of sawmills and of logs trimmed at felling sites by de-barking machines is measured in metres. The smell of the sulphate mills is measured in kilometres; it is called the smell of wealth (so too is that of the malodorous mink, fox and racoon). Beyond the great cauldrons where pulped timber stews and ferments are the laboratories where the exotic scents of an ever-increasing range of by-products are heavy in the controlled atmosphere. Fermentation is a feature of Finland. Illegal distillation doubtless continues, although the smell is rarely detectable, except perhaps in the vicinity of a *puliukko* or city drunkard.

Contrastingly, the smell of fermenting silage belongs to most farms. Unlike the smell of hay, which eddying currents of air can carry a long distance, that of silage is restricted to the barn. It has become one with the smells of the byre, which have been endured for so many centuries that they are commonly disregarded. The faint smell of pesticides and herbicides is as inescapable as those of the wayside sprays for laying dust on the diminishing length of unsurfaced highways, of the preservatives absorbed by all manner of wooden buildings and released by summer heat, of the oily smells of ships' chandlers' stores and the paint of boatyards.

Floral smells are recalled with much pleasure — fugitive essences more subtle than the heavy scents of Finland's ubiquitous flower shops. There are pools of scent in the early summer woodlands offered by lilies-of-the-valley or by cowslips — surely none larger than those in the meadows of Nagu in Turku archipelago. Lilac adds its faint perfume to every town park and country garden. Honeysuckle has a more intoxicating odour. The spicy smell of phlox and the heavy scent of the linden tree come later: so too that of ling on sunny heathland. The smell of rapeseed has added a new element to the countryside. It replaces that of the nearly vanished buckwheat and the dusty smell of the ryefield in bloom (*heilimöidä* — a deliciously distinctive Finnish word). Other plants wait for their scents to be released by pressure — bruised juniper and the aromatic bog myrtle. D.H. Lawrence identified all these 'chemical exhalations' as an integral part of his 'spirit of place'. But, then, so much academic botany has become chemistry since the days of Linnaeus's taxonomy.

A sense of surfaces

The nineteenth-century cartoonist A.W. Linsén depicted Elias
Lönnrot setting out in search of oral poetry as a somewhat spiderish figure
striding through thin pine woods in his bare feet. The outside world
doubtless assumed that this was because he could not afford shoes. In fact,
there were plenty of heath cobblers who would have been only too
delighted to supply the needs of a by-no-means impecunious medical
doctor. Many Finns choose to go barefoot in summer — 'barefoot days'
they used to be called in some parts of the country and traditionally they
began on Ascension Day. It is pleasant to feel the touch of *terra firma*
through the soles of the feet — or at least through the partly hardened
soles. There is pleasure in the contrasting sensations of moist earth, warm
rock (smooth, rough, rippled), cool wet sand, a carpet of pine needles,
spongy sphagnum, encrusted lichens, cushioned moss (Larin Kyösti called
moss the ultimate enemy of the Finn). Bare feet are an invitation to
stinging insects — even to poisonous snakes, especially in the archipelagos, but the risks are slight.

Surfaces have a tactile appeal. The smoothness of a prehistoric soapstone
relic in Mariehamn is recalled: so, too, is that of time-worn statuary in
several medieval churches. A similar smoothness characterises the products
of early horn-makers, the warm flanks of tall tiled stoves and the leathery
surfaces of birch-bark wear — shoes, back pack, indeed an entire suit in
Österbotten museum. The pleasurable feel of the satin-like surface of
finely honed wood is enhaced by the possibility of seeing time rippling
through its annual rings. The textures of woven fabrics have their own
feel — smooth linen cloth contrasting with coarse linen sheets, hand-
mangled instead of ironed. The rag-and-straw paper made in many little
mills in earlier days was rough too; the quill pen cannot have moved too
easily over its surface. (Were the quills from the feathers of the wild goose?
When did the domesticated goose arrive in Finland?) There is the feel of
furs — silky mink, stiff bear, rough reindeer pelts, fluffy sheepskin. The
clammy feel of prickly-finned, slippery fish is inseparable from the experience of Finland.

A different sensation is the crackle of electricity discharged as wood or
metal is touched on a fine, dry winter day — the kind of day when hair
clings to the comb and almost emits its own spark. The same type of
weather causes an intense tingling in the nose, quite different from the
momentary tingling of the flesh on rolling in the snow following the sweat
of the winter sauna.

Finland is not without a variety of biting creatures that seek human
surfaces. For Linnaeus the mosquitos and insufferable clouds of midges
transformed Lapland into a 'green hell'. In Enontekiö personal protection

was sought against them in a virtual bridal veil. As elsewhere, wasps do their best to reduce the enjoyment of picnics. The elk fly, laying its eggs in the ears and nostrils of its unfortunate host, has penetrated into south-east Finland. It is easily picked up from the spoor of the elk when mushrooming; then it clings tenaciously and irritatingly to the hair and is resistant to the heat of the sauna. The bed bug, red devil instrusive from the other side of the border and so graphically described a century ago by the lively Mrs Alec Tweedie, has met its Waterloo.

Matters of taste

It is a matter of taste, but many would say that Finnish bread is the best in the world. 'Give us this day our daily bread', according to one Karelian husbandman, implies bread that is made daily — if not daily, his wife seems quite happy to bake several times a week. There is no ceiling pole in their home on which the round flat bread could be stored for future use. Bowls of rising dough and the smell of baking in many homes remain sufficiently widespread to keep Finnish bakeries on their toes producing high-quality wheaten bread, rye bread, French bread, hard bread, crisp bread, flat bread, Åland black bread and sweet bread (*pulla*). With such an abundance of irresistible bread available, it is difficult to realise that within living memory in less accessible parts of Finland supplies of bread grain were sometimes so meagre that substitutes had to be found to eke them out. The pulverised phloem of trees was among the principal surrogates employed, and so-called bark bread was the product. It can still be seen — under glass in museums, flint hard.

Potatoes provide another daily dish. Two centuries ago, there was an intensive potato campaign, the like of which has probably been seen in no other country. Potatoes were preached from the pulpit and praised by poets. Seed potatoes were distributed freely to farmers through the agency of the Swedish crown. Potatoes may still be stored in rural areas in boulder-built bunkers and in special cellars beneath a trapdoor in the living-room floor. There is still something of a ceremony about potato lifting, although the potato holiday has disappeared. At their most choice they await the customer in the boats that arrive at Helsinki's south harbour. 'Give us this day our daily potatoes', but remember that dill must accompany them, pungent dill.

Butter goes with both bread and potatoes. The quality of Finnish dairy products cannot be exceeded. In the late nineteenth century, Finnish butter was too good to export as 'Russian butter', so it was shipped covertly to Denmark and exported as Danish. 'The greatness and goodness of their cheeses' was already praised by Olaus Magnus in the mid-sixteenth century. The cartwheels of Finnish Emmenthal can out-

Emmenthal the product of the Jura (both Swiss and French) in the international market. Cheeses are a matter of taste. Not everyone enjoys the rubbery Ostrobothnian pancake-flat cheeses. Nor are the milk cultures always relished. Finns conceived their own varieties before the days of yoghurt — smooth *viili* (*filmjölk*), *kokkeli-piimä* (a lumpy product) and *pitkäpiimä* (*långmjölk*), which when poured from a jug may need to be clipped at the spout. And milk goes with porridge — oat, rye, rice, buckwheat — and pink whortleberry beloved of children.

Wildwood and waters yield plenty to stimulate the palate. The harvest of berries, many common to Scandinavia and Russia, is unrivalled. There are blueberries (which give their name to the *vaccinium* forest type), cowberries or *puolukka* (retaining their piquancy without preservatives), cranberries and vitamin-rich but pippy cloudberries (the gifts of the bogland), precious *mesimarja* (the fast-disappearing *Rubus arcticus*, which unhappily resists cultivation). There are wild raspberries, diminutive currants and gooseberries, especially in the islands, clustered seathorne berries (amber droplets on great grey bushes along the Ostrobothnian coast). There are rose hips for soup and rowan — sweet rowan, too — for preserves. There are wild strawberries, more flavoursome if less fleshy than those cultivated in Savo. Riistavesi hospitality is remembered for an unrivalled compôte of Finnish wild berries.

To the berries must be added the fungi — a score of edible types to be gathered before the frost reduces them to a pulp. Some will be salted, some dried, some pickled. Everyone has a favourite variety — and secret harvesting area. Most sought after is the *chanterelle* — crocus-yellow, nestling in twigs and fallen leaves, almost dancing in magic circles (unforgettably prolific in Lemi). The dead fly mushroom, *Agorica*, crimson and white spotted, has been known to have been consumed deliberately to produce hallucinations. And, as if there are not enough fungi in Finland, Volga mushrooms are imported by health faddists from across the border, where it is believed that the juices that they produce, when suspended Medusa-like in a jar, prolong life.

The waters produce their seasonal harvests. Lines dropped through ice-holes leave the fish no winter rest. Sweetest of all is the *siika* or white fish (*corregonus*), at its best smoked. Salmon farming makes up any deficiency of wild salmon, but if the stalls of Helsinki's fishwives are anything to go by, there still seems an abundance of the wild variety. Salted salmon (*gravlax*) takes precedence in Finnish taste over smoked salmon. As summer begins to fade, the crayfish brings a lobster-red touch to the table. In the autumn, a virtual *silakka* or Baltic herring festival is celebrated. In Helsinki as many as two dozen herring-boats may arrive from as far afield as Kökar and Kotka. A market is set up on the waterfront. In tubs and jars, smoked, salted and pickled herring are displayed — pickled herring flavoured with spices, tomato, lemon, curry or garlic. And troops of schoolchildren join the crowd that comes to enjoy the seasonal festival.

In the lakes there are plenty of pike waiting to be trapped. Around Kuopio, the dimunitive *muikku*, cousin to the trout, provides the perfect ingredient for the redoubtable Mrs Partanen's *kalakukko*, or fish pie. Smoked elvers are available from the delicatessen for those who like them.

Variety is extended to the bill of fare by Friday's pea soup and pancakes, by the springtime bird soup (*fågelsoppa*) of the outer islands, by regional specialities such as Karelian *piirakka* and *blini*, by seasonal specialities such as sticky Eastertide *mämmi* and Christmas ham.

The woods also provide game. Domesticated reindeer in Lapland yield their own range of products. It is difficult to eat the delectable reindeer tongue without a twinge of conscience. Contrastingly, there are memories of an encounter with ominously irridescent salted reindeer in an Enontekiö retreat. Wild deer are available for shooting (called hunting), but it is the elk that takes precedence. The woodcock is much esteemed. The wild duck is favoured more than the wild goose. In the eighteenth century Pehr Kalm sought unsuccessfully to naturalise wild rice, *Zinzania aquatica*, to accompany roast duck as in North America.

And, since a dry throat is a dumb throat (*Ei kumaja kuiva kurkku*), there must be appropriate beverages. Water has not always been as palatable as it might be. Finnish beers, brewed since Kalevalan times, are first-rate. *Kalja* — small beer, perhaps — is not for everyone. *Koskenkorva* or Finnish vodka is an indispensible accompaniment of the cold table. Finnish wines — and the sweet, berry-based liqueurs — are a matter of taste. *Sima* or mead, slightly effervescent, is commonly drunk on the first of May. Less usual is *mahla*, the birch-sap beverage. It is hard to find a bad cup of Finnish coffee: in its consistently high quality it must lead the world. A Colombian ambassador does his best to ensure that there is no deterioration. Equally high is the quality of inexpensive wines sold by *Alkoholiliike*, the state alcohol monopoly. Simply because of the quantity that it purchases, suppliers dare not produce anything other than the best. High prices discourage the drinking of spirits.

Pere syöp, pöytä laulaa (The family eats, the table sings), says an old Savo proverb. Often it groans rather than sings beneath the burden of the Epicurean *voileipäpöytä* or *smörgåsbord*. Piling Pelion on Ossa, there are also the delectable cakes and sweetmeats that bring renown to the name of century-old Fazer. With the increasing number of young Finns learning their trade at hotel and restaurant schools — bringing happy memories of Sunday lunches at Puijonsarvi above Kuopio — the future of Finnish eating and drinking is in safe hands.

A sixth sense

John Ruskin wrote of 'feeling a country in all its fullness'. Such feeling, rooted in the shifting combinations of the five senses, is unique to individuals. The evocations that the senses yield often amount to more than the sum of the separate components. The bundle of sensations felt in Finland — a synthesis in its way and the response of an outsider over a particular span of time — raises questions. First, to what extent does a Finn respond in the same way as a foreigner? Secondly, are there (better perhaps were there) sensations felt by Finns or some Finns that lie beyond the experience of an outsider? Are the eyes of Finland's country people sharper and their ears more sensitively attuned to the sounds of nature than those who have been removed from the land for several generations? What are the sources of the 'earth spirit' (*maahenki*) that binds the Finnish farmer to his plot? Is there one of Herder's 'other senses', a sixth sense, retained by some Finns for some reason in some places?

The case of the reindeer-herding Lapps supports the notion. Close association with animal instinct appears to transmit something to the human subject. Certainly, there are enough strange tales of their experiences to warrant a measure of belief in the possession by at least some Lapps of a sixth sense. Nor is it to be separated from a residue of the animistic, which is a quality that has lingered among them longer than among most Europeans. Furthermore, the historical confusion of Lapp and Finn (more correctly, Finnmarker) has led to the association of necromancy with Finns — an attribute which, through several centuries, authors of fiction have sustained and extended. There is a related point. Even within living memory there have been many Finns who have know the pangs of hunger. And hunger, especially when linked with particular dietary deficiencies, can produce unusual chemical reactions which may well lead to strange mental conditions. There is historical evidence that it led to the genocide practised during the great famine of 1696–7. Certainly there was more than a residue of belief in necromancy in parts of the country in the eighteenth century, with a prelate reporting of Karelians that many of them were caught by it 'like birds in a snare or fish on a hook'. Hallucination and hunger, shamanism and revelation have hung together — even hallucination and sectarianism, as epitomised by Tyko Sallinen's canvas of the *Devil's Dream*. All this, though speculative and intangible, offers a splendid hunting-ground for social psychologists.

To a parallel area of speculation belongs the Finnish reaction to Russia — at the personal as well as the national level. It is as though an automatic pilot were operating — perhaps, a better metaphor, as though there was something that enters through the pores of the nation resulting from generations of existence on the Russian border. Some explain the reaction as the product of intuition — a sixth sense: for others, such as the Swiss observer Andreas Dorfner, it is nothing more than a neurosis.

Be all this as it may, personal experience suggests that in Finland, chance encounters and coincidences occur with greater frequency than in most countries. The encounters often seem as though they are enchanted experiences. More mundanely, the explanation may be that Finns are more thin upon the ground, that they are increasingly on the move, and that the possibility of paths crossing is therefore higher than in many places.

But the experience is not confined to people. Papers and documents of research interest have a habit of seeking out their searchers rather than *vice versa*. Again, the explanation may be that they are not so abundant or so widely scattered as in many countries.

Finally, there is the uncanny personal feeling that more people in Finland than elsewhere seem to know what you are thinking before you speak. Perhaps the *frisson* is simply the strange perceptual feeling of a foreigner. Whatever the explanation, it would be pleasant to think that a sixth sense has not altogether been extinguished from a civilised world.

4

ENCOUNTERS WITH THE PAST

'. . . they are not papers, but lives of men, of provinces. . . . as
I breathed on their dust, I saw them rise up.'
(Jules Michelet, *History of France*, 1835–47)

A kind of truancy

Personal encounters with the past of Finland have taken many forms.
There is a recollection of Matts Dreijer, standing by the memorial called
Tingstenen in Saltvik, back turned to what was once a creek where
medieval trading vessels moored, speculating on the stave church that
preceded the thirteenth-century stone building and suggesting (not
without evidence) that there might have been a second Birka in Åland.
There is a memory of a sunny afternoon spent fascinated by a collection of
artifacts — glass bottles and porcelain, fragments of corroded copper and
shell-encrusted cannons — rescued by a Kotka dentist and his diver friends
from the wrecks of vessels sunk in the battle of Svensksund (Ruotsinsalmi).
It was remembered again when the *Wasa* and *Mary Rose* were lifted and
there was talk of the possibility of raising the oaken hull of a Swedish man-
of-war or of a frigate such as the Russians built of Siberian larch . . . But,
then, who might claim ownership?

There are reflections as well as recollections. It is a pity that tape-
recorders only began to be common possessions about the time that many
who might have contributed to oral history were passing away. The pity is
greater because an emerging interest in industrial archaeology was simultaneously investing a host of relics with an aura of romance. Thus, within
the passage of the post-war generation, the last Finns have died who might
have dredged lake ore for the Karelian iron works at Pankakoski, Lieksa or
Möhkö. It is the same with the nameless builders who cemented the
glaucous green slag into the foundations of homes in and around
Dahlsbruk to glint to the memory of defunct foundries. There must also
have been octogenarians who were once smoke-blackened like the children
in Eero Järnefelt's painting as they engaged in the practice of *kaskenpoltto*
or swidden. Forty years ago, in parts of south-east Finland, it was still
possible to detect from the vegetation where the woodland had been
burn-beaten.

To the old-established ethnographic interest in such practices and artifacts the post-war years have added an increased interest in the story of other

everyday things. It has been interesting to see the ransacking of family albums and commercial archives with unexpectedly fruitful results for the history of Finnish photography. Nor need more be said of the film archive than that it is rich enough to merit the foundation of a museum of cinematography, especially since Finnish films have acquired an international reputation. The story of private as well as public entertainments provides a chapter in Finnish history which is highly diverting. Thus, the formal studies of Ester-Margaret von Frenckell have been complemented with exploration of the nooks and crannies of the entertainment world by Sven Hirn, with circuses performing in settlements where, in years of famine, bread itself might be hard to come by.

The experience of Finland is inseparable from the study of its history — and the encounter with its historians. Personal concern has been with social and economic history rather than political. Encounters have been rather more fortuitous than planned, and they have followed byways rather than highways. They have also been the excursions of an amateur who, at a time of increasing professionalism among historians, has trespassed into certain fields, partly because they appear to have been overlooked, partly because they have overlapped with his own discipline. Investigations have sometimes provided introductions to Finns who have offered new perspectives on their country's past: they have also led to a few who have become virtually a part of history itself.

For many foreigners who have worked or studied in post-war Finland, the absence of a comprehensive review of the cultural and social relations between Finland and their home countries must have been evident. The relationships between Finland and the United Kingdom, the German-speaking countries of Europe, France, Italy, Denmark, the Netherlands — even Russia — all merit a monograph. Juhani Paasivirta's partly autobiographical study of the relations between Finland and the United States of America offers a possible model.

At a personal level, the temptation to adopt the study of Anglo-Finnish relations has been difficult to resist. Inevitably, it began as serendipity. The hobby soon became a kind of work, contrasting with the more formal research which became a kind of play. Sometimes, it competed for time with it: sometimes, it altered its direction. Moreover, archival material touching upon Anglo-Finnish relations began to seek out the seeker as well as being sought.

In the process, individuals began to rise from their papers and to invite fuller acquaintance. Some emerged logically. Thus, sooner or later, anyone with an interest in botany would encounter Pehr Kalm, topographer and natural husbandman, favourite student of Carl Linnaeus. Kalm was to prove a kindred spirit, if a dry stick. Some individuals were encountered by happy accident — hence Johan Jacob von Julin, a warm and enterprising character who was a founding father of Finland. Sometimes, the sheer frequency with which their publications made an impact called for a fuller acquaintance — hence Zacharias Topelius. At first it seemed that devoting precious time to these individuals when the focus of research lay elsewhere was a kind of truancy. It engendered a measure of unease until each, obligingly, provided his own excuse for being incoporated in the historico-geographical research field itself.

A sortie into Anglo-Finnish relations

In 1948, an invitation to give a paper to the Roscoe Society of the University of Liverpool prompted an inquiry into old British travel books on Finland. Edward Clarke's *Travels in Scandinavia and Finland* (belatedly published in 1820 as the third of six volumes of his travels) started an interest in topographical literature on Finland which has borne continuous fruit. Clarke's *Travels* and William Otter's *Life and Remains of E.D. Clarke* (London, 1825) incorporate the best statements on Finland down to their time, though they are well complemented by the *Travels* of the 'Italian gentleman' Joseph Acerbi in 1799–1800. Clarke travelled in the company of three other men from Jesus College, Cambridge — William Otter, Thomas Malthus and John Marten Cripps. As the most distinguished of them, Malthus naturally aroused expectations. A personal inquiry made in Jesus College library for a presumed diary by Malthus covering his journey north yielded no result; although his somewhat disappointing diary for Norway and Sweden was later discovered and published by a descendant. Did Malthus keep a diary on the Finnish leg of his journey? It would have been unusual had he not done so. And are there Otter archives in Chichester cathedral? None of the volumes of Clarke's *Travels*, much-prized collectors' items, has been republished, but there is a translation in Finnish by Jorma Ojala of the journey through Finland. It is a handsome well-annotated volume. A brief but lively correspondence rekindled an old interest. A search for Clarke's birthplace revealed that it had been pulled down during the expansion of the seaside resort of Eastbourne. Contrastingly, the Georgian residence of 'the Sussex worthy' John Marten Cripps, Stanton Manor near Lewes, is a listed building with an entry in the *Victoria County History of Sussex*.

Stanton Manor is located within gunshot of the old gaol where Finnish prisoners-of-war were housed after they had been transported from the fortress of Bomarsund in Åland during the Crimean War. A personal interest in the topic was first generated in a Liverpool context. On his departure from the University in 1949, Cyril Northcote Parkinson was kind enough to present to me his volumes of the *Naval Records Society* covering the Baltic campaigns of 1854–5. The naval operations around the

Finnish coast, which gave rise to folksong as well as to folklore, called for centennial celebration. *Oolannin sota*, as the episode was popularly known in Finland, resulted in one of Marta Hirn's memorable picture-books. A pilgrimage was made in her company to the old gaol to photograph the cells in which the prisoners had lived and the memorial to those who died in the churchyard of St John sub Castro. Amusingly, the Lewes Society persuaded the Russian embassy to pay for the restoration of the obelisk, the names on which had suffered serious weathering. Attention was also claimed by the memorabilia at the National Maritime Museum, from the uniform of Admiral (Black Charlie) Napier to the drawers filled with sketches by the war artist Oswald Brierly. Since then, the Baltic campaigns have yielded a colourful volume by Basil Greenhill and Ann Giffard, although there remain many parcels tied with pink tape in the naval archives of the Public Record Office which must tell complementary and supplementary stories to those that the authors have so vividly brought to light.

A related sortie into the activities of the Peace Party could scarcely be avoided. It led to the Society of Friends and the records of their London headquarters. The active endeavours of their supporters to compensate the Finnish coastal inhabitants for the damage that their property suffered from British naval incursions as well as their later attempts to bring succour to the famine-fringes of Finland are a forgotten episode. There are memories of turning over papers in the then windy and icy garret of Kuopio's now immaculate city hall searching unsuccessfully for references to members of the British Society of Friends who came bringing assistance. The loose heaps of papers on the floor contained much fascinating material to attract a foreigner — not least the copies of permits given to Russian peddlers who travelled into Savo from Archangel and Olonetz. The search for the Quaker visitors ended successfully in church archives — some as far afield as Hyrynsalmi.

Among those sympathetic to the lot of the Finns during the Baltic campaigns was John Good of Hull, owner of a brig which traded with the Ostrobothnian ports. An inquiry after the commercial archives of the company that he founded led by good fortune to his diary which had escaped the destruction of the Scale Lane office during the war years. The names of his trader friends in Jakobstad, Brahestad and Uleåborg (as he called them) aroused a curiosity over what complementary material might exist in the three ports. Among others, it led to the substantial files of *Malmska handelshuset*, the trading company of his friend Pehr Malm — files explored with much profit by Oscar Nikula. The material whetted the appetite sufficiently to explore the archives of other companies trading with Britain. The files of the colourful Hackman Company of Viborg (Viipuri) from the period 1750–1820, except during the

Napoleonic Wars, provided evidence of dealings with a full hundred British trading companies.

It is worth recalling that John Good's brig was tying up at Ostrobothnian wharves at the same time that the Scottish cleric John Paterson was serving as secretary of the British and Foreign Bible Society in St Petersburg. His *Book for every Land* (1858) has commercial as well as ecclesiastical anecdotes. It was he who pointed James Finlayson to the potentialities of the water power site at Tampere for a cotton mill. It is unfortunate that the script in the copy-books of the Society, which contain correspondence referring to Finland, has faded so badly that that it is all but indecipherable. The Finlayson mill, together with John Barker's mill at Turku, developed its own Anglo-Finnish network, not least on the distaff side. Through her educational work, Mrs Finlayson kept in touch with a number of friends, among them the Quakers of the Shusharry settlement near St Petersburg. Casting an eye over the Finlayson papers for further references to the British connection, a bundle of letters came to light which are remembered not only for their content but for a pencilled note attached to them. This stated that they were being put in order as the guns of the Civil War were firing round the factory.

Other wars and times of stress have linked Finland and Britain. There was a British fleet in the Baltic during the Great Northern War. A British observer, Admiral Sir John Norris, was present at the signing of the Treaty of Nystad (Uusikaupunki) in 1721. Again, it is curious how Finland breeds coincidences. The best description of Finland in English from the time appeared in the *Atlas Maritimus et Commercialis* (1728) which was dedicated to the astronomer Edmund Halley as well as to Sir John Norris. The text is generally attributed to Daniel Defoe (who also wrote a little-known novel about a Finnish warlock). An invitation from Benenden School in Kent to talk about Finland revealed that it had been the home of Sir John Norris and that he was buried in the nearby village church. Quite by chance, the final draft of a paper on Norris was being prepared at the time. Nor was that all. Uncannily, a painting of the three lady founders of the School greets visitors as they enter the vestibule. It is by Kenneth Green, a friend who for a number of years painted portraits all round Finland.

While the British fleet was making intermittent excursions into the Baltic during the early eighteenth century, several merchants of Finnish provenance were establishing themselves in London. Prominent among them was Thomas Spieker, who contributed generously to the completion of the city's first Swedish church. It was dedicated to the Swedish queen Ulrika Eleonora and located east of the Tower. The names of other Finns in the Swedish community can be gleaned from its records. Gustavus Brander, a younger cousin, inherited much of the Spieker estate. Brander, a founder member of the British Museum and a friend of Daniel Solander, was visited by many Swedes and Finns. His retirement home still stands close to Christchurch Priory in Hampshire, at the east end of which a coat-of-arms marks his association with the church. The chain of Finnish connections continues, because Solander went with Sir Joseph Banks and his company of philosophers on Captain Cook's voyage to the Pacific. In turn, Solander took with him Herman Diedrich Spöring, a young Finn who had been trained as an instrument-maker in London. Spöring died in the South Seas; he is remembered in an island which bears his name off the coast of New Zealand.

Redolent of another time of stress, and remarkable to see, is a Finnish document which must be unique in Europe. It is the *Pro Finlandia* address that the Tsar Nicholas II refused to receive. The petition, signed by more than 1,000 leading European representatives of the arts and sciences, urged restraint in the political pressure being exerted on Finland. British signatories included Thomas Hardy and Florence Nightingale (long after many people thought she was dead). Newspapers from the time also stick in the mind, with their blacked-out columns identifying censorship and their page after page of Fennicised surnames (*nimenmuuttoja*), which were another means of registering anti-Russian protest.

Sometimes, in the search for Anglo-Finnish links, family chests were made available. At Åminnefors, they revealed papers concerning the first school founded for Finnish-speaking children according to the pedagogical principles of the Lancaster Bell schools in Britain. An old guest book recorded observations by English visitors. On September 11, 1837, Joseph Travers wrote that he had 'visited the mine and sincerely wishes that none of his friends may break their necks which there is some danger in doing'. Access to the Armfelt papers was sought in order to inquire into Alexander Armfelt's education in Britain. It was, according to his father, a safer place than 'the Sodom and Gomorrah of revolutionary France'. Alexander's correspondence reveals him to have been an exuberant teenager during his Edinburgh days: '*Trois mois et un siècle de souvenirs*', he wrote. Replies from an adolescent lady-friend suggest that his memories were as much amatory as academic. 'I would have my son grow up with the plough in one hand: if need be, the sword in the other', commented his father. In the event, neither was employed, but Alexander Armfelt proved a good servant of the Grand Duchy. . . . And, looking for British links in the family chest at nearby Angelniemi, there was an accidental encounter with letters to Siri von Essen from August Strindberg. They were discreetly left unread. What has happened to them since the death of the owner, the agronomist Wava von Essen?

Very different from the sturdy family chests was a humble suitcase deposited at the library of Åbo Akademi and filled with as yet uncatalogued letters received by Alma Söderhjelm. It contained an invitation from the year 1911 to the inaugural meeting of the Anglo-Finnish Society at 8 Holland Park Avenue, London. The card was enclosed with a letter from her friend, Aino Malmberg, a robust Finnish activist.

Aino Malmberg was a lively correspondent. She was an acceptable recruit to Fabian and feminist circles during her extended London sojourn. There were weekends with Mrs Despard, 'one of the leaders of the women's movement', in the company of the Ramsay MacDonalds; with Lady Burne-Jones at Rottingdean, 'meeting W. Morris and Watts at every step'. There was dinner with Prince Kropotkin ('very clever, but an absolute boor') and George Bernard Shaw (whose *Devil's Disciple* and *Man and Superman* she set about translating into Finnish). She lunched with Lady Balfour at her club; among political activists she consorted with Keir Hardie. All was undertaken to further the Finnish cause. She undertook grand provincial lecture tours, sorted out possible Russian spies and informers, and courted the editors of newspapers and journals. She also passed on an extraordinary titbit from a letter that she had received from W.T. Stead dated November 30, 1909. It was at this time that the scientist Sir Oliver Lodge's spiritualist séances were in full vigour, and Stead wrote to her: 'I do not know what your views are on the spirit world, but I have received several messages purporting to come from Catherine the Great, who is excessively disturbed on the subject of Finland'.

Sometimes it has been no more than an English name which has aroused curiosity and set a long trail in motion. Wanderings in the old cemetery on the outskirts of Turku led to tombstones associated with the evidently British family of Cowie. An enquiry into the origins of the Turku shipyards revealed them to be linked with the name of a British engineer, Robert Fithie, some 250 years ago, with the Cowies taking over a century later and being finally followed by the Crichtons. At this point, the Wärtsilä concern enters the story, because it acquired the Crichton Vulcan yards at Turku. The Wärtsilä archive contains an autobiographical essay by William Crichton, a Leith engineer, who joined the Turku firm of Ericsson and Cowie in 1850, in 'Russian Finland', as British engineers described it. Hence Crichton's comment, 'Thus, a long cherished wish was fulfilled, namely of emigrating to Russia'.

Ironically, the wish was more correctly fulfilled through the exceptional circumstances of the Crimean War, with the experiences of William Crichton providing another illustration of the remarkable episodes that sprang from it. Crichton, as an enemy alien, was removed from Åbo ('politely' was the operative word) to a jail in St Petersburg, but was soon released to reside with his cousin Sir William Crichton, sometime physician to Nicholas I. He was appointed to post in a government engineering plant, married in the English church, stayed at the Kolpino works till 1862 and, suitably bemedalled, returned to Åbo to take up his engineering pursuits with John Julin. Once again, friends encountered in independent Anglo-Finnish contexts were brought together. . . . Nor does the link stop there. The branches of the Crichton family tree stretch out to pre-war London, where Greta Hinke, a direct descendant, was among the regular hostesses of the pre-war Anglo-Finnish Society.

The demise of the Wärtsilä concern is sad for those who have been familiar with its name through forty years of Finland's commercial and industrial history — especially so for those who have known its ancestry.

The engineering theme prompted a visit to the Saimaa Canal archive, most of which is in Mikkeli. The model for the canal had been the Trollhättan Canal in Sweden, where James Brindley had been the consulting engineer. The archive, transported under virtual siege conditions from Viipuri during the war, was eventually housed in the Mikkeli accommodation that had been blasted out of the rock to serve as Mannerheim's wartime headquarters — a memorable place in which to sift through the letter books and reports from the constructional period.

By this time, too, Finland had a network of foreign vice-consuls. In Helsinki, the British appointed a somewhat modestly-paid officer — Consul Crowe (who had a more famous brother in North Norway). Foreign Office papers enabled the birth of the British consular system in the Grand Duchy to be traced. Mostly they covered the expanding trade, from virtual Noah's Arks of farm animals to equipment for installing coal-gas supplies, from machine parts for the sugar refineries to engine drivers to teach the novices who took charge of the first Finnish railway line. Since the Second World War, honorary Finnish vice-consuls have proliferated.

A student of natural husbandry

While Robert Fithie was engaged in developing a shipyard at Åbo, a zealous young Finn was on his way to join the students of Carl Linnaeus in Uppsala. He was Pehr Kalm (1717–79), who is better known today than two generations ago. In 1948, an antiquarian bookseller produced a copy of the translation by the geologist Joseph Lucas of *Kalm's Account of his visit to England on the way to America in 1748* (1892). The *Visit to England* struck a direct connection between Finland and the Hertfordshire Chilterns. Kalm's legacy of observations and comments are recalled with every passage through the countryside where he stayed during the three springtime weeks of his visit. His purpose was to enquire into the character of farming in a part of England which his patron, Baron Sten Carl Bielke, believed to be the most advanced in all the country. In particular, Kalm was required to visit William Ellis, a resident of Little Gaddesden, an improver of agricultural equipment and the author of a number of celebrated husbandry books.

In his topographical account of the rural scene and its inhabitants, Kalm produced a statement unequalled by any English observer of the time. His observations are the more entertaining because of his treatment of everyday objects and activities. For example, no British observer would have considered describing in detail (almost tedious detail) the procedures involved in planting a hedgerow or building a hayrick. The diary begins each day with precise weather recordings — the temperatures being in the measurements of his friend Anders Celsius — which are unique for the area from the mid-eighteenth century.

It was the opinion of the English poet Thomas Gray as well as of Linnaeus himself that a word or two written on the spot were worth a cartload of recollections. Kalm heeded the advice. He may be imagined writing up his miscellaneous observations nightly by candlelight with a quill pen on rag paper, reporting in a plain puritan style, though not without the occasional memorable metaphor (the thorny wild plum 'a wool thief', the hawthorn sucker 'an arrant knave') and wry aphorism ('A fat hen lays no eggs'). Kalm was both empiricist and theorist. He debated the origins of chalk and flints and teased out the plant species in a bundle of hay with equal effect. Above all, he was a practical husbandman — his motto *experiendo non conjectando*.

Kalm is constantly a part of the personal experience of Finland because the curiosity aroused by his English journey generated an urge to follow the trail of his life and work. The fine church of St Maria where he was incumbent in his later years has been regularly visited and, happily, it has not yet been swallowed up by the expanding bricks and mortar of Turku. A plain memorial to Kalm has been placed on the wall beside the altar, facing the rows of smoky blue pews. Across the road is the bosky garden of his vicarage, with an ancient bowed tree, Kalm's linden. Above the vicarage door is a plaque inscribed '*Att spara skogen, landets rikedom*'.* There are memories of coffee in the garden with Jaakko Haavio, sometime vicar of St Marie, and of perusing the church books from Kalm's incumbency.

Maria church is mentally linked with the medieval church at Little Gaddesden. William Ellis lived at Church Farm round the corner from the flint church itself; Kalm stayed at the *Robin Hood*, the village inn now a private residence. Kalm was not as impressed by Ellis as he expected to be. His candid comments, which have been read aloud to generations of students as they have halted beside the church on Chiltern excursions, are almost strong enough to induce Ellis to rise from his nearby grave. By a coincidence, the Church Farm which Kalm visited is owned by a family of Meads. It was also the refuge for Swedish friends from the vulnerable Luton factory of SKF† during the war years.

* Save the forests, the country's wealth.
† The Swedish ball-bearings manufacturer Svenska Kullager-fabriken.

The several square miles of Hertfordshire over which Kalm walked and the houses where he talked might well be called 'Kalm country'. The landscape retains many features little changed since his time. There are woods of beech and oak and common land, ancient hedgerows bordering flinty fields and unusual groves of boxwood. On the lower benches of what he called the 'frighteningly high' chalk escarpment, sheep are folded. The ridged and furrowed land in the clay vale below, a relic of medieval selions which he carefully measured, may still be seen. On the Totternhoe ridge, which thrusts into the vale, chalk rock used to be mined. Kalm's diary contains the fullest statement from the eighteenth century of the operations of the chalk rock mines. They are sealed today, but the lime burning at a nearby kiln continues.

From rural England and metropolitan London, Kalm embarked on a six weeks' passage to the New World. The landfall on the banks of the Delaware anticipated the longer and more purposeful part of his journal, which was also to prove the most celebrated. It was a memorable experience to follow in his wake from the old Swedish church in Philadelphia through upstate New York and along the shores of Lake Ontario to Niagara; Kalm's description of the Falls appeared in the *Gentleman's Magazine* in 1751. Not least, it has been rewarding to follow Kalm's route into Quebec province. His topographical observations on New France from 1749 are unrivalled by those of any foreigner. In this context, it has been exciting to follow to its conclusion the labour of love undertaken by the Abbé Guy Béthune and Jacques Rousseau of their richly annotated French translation of Kalm's Quebec diary.

The personal associations with Kalm's name are manifold. Among the first was a lecture on Kalm to the Warrington Philosophical Society in the original Academy building where the early teachers included John

---

Fig. 5. A page from the diary of Pehr Kalm

Pehr Kalm kept a near-daily diary during his journey in England on the way to North America. This entry, from the copy of the diary discovered in 1899, is headed 'England: Ivinghoe in Buckinghamshire, April 5'. (Courtesy University Library, Helsinki)

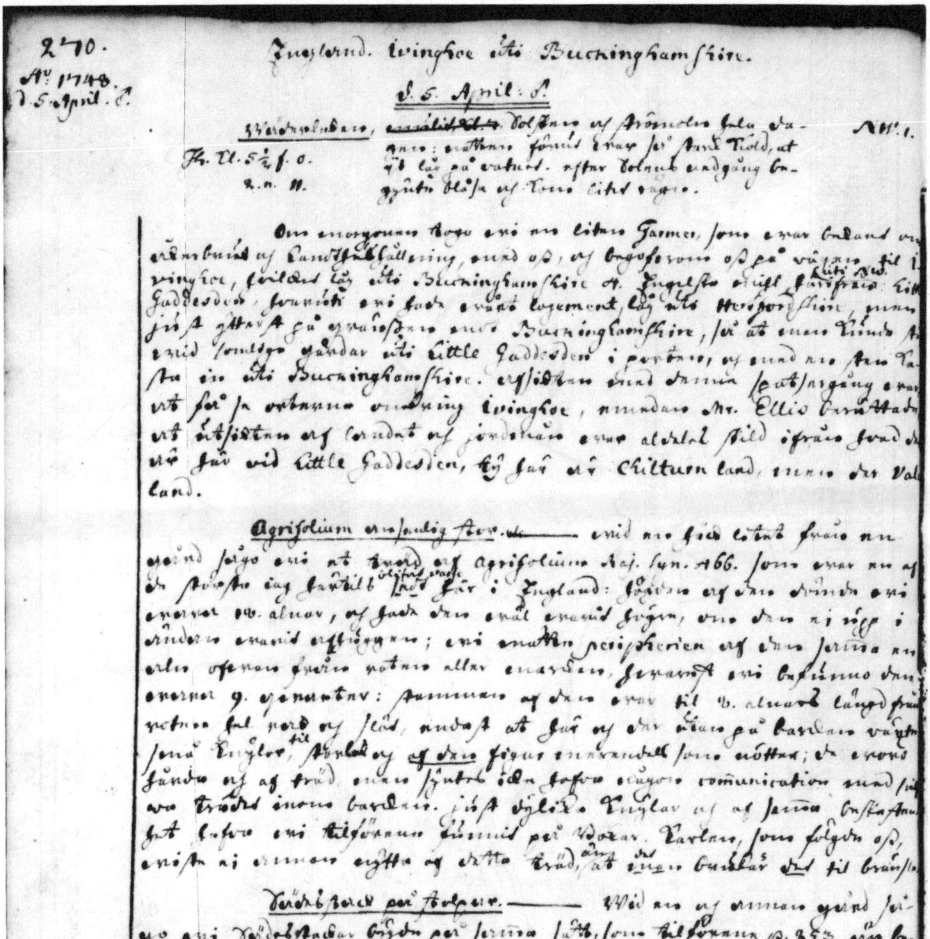

270.

A:o 1748
d 5 April. E

England. Ivinghoe uti Buckinghamshire.

d. 5 April.

Agrifolium

Wärderäd på stolpar.

Plättbröd.

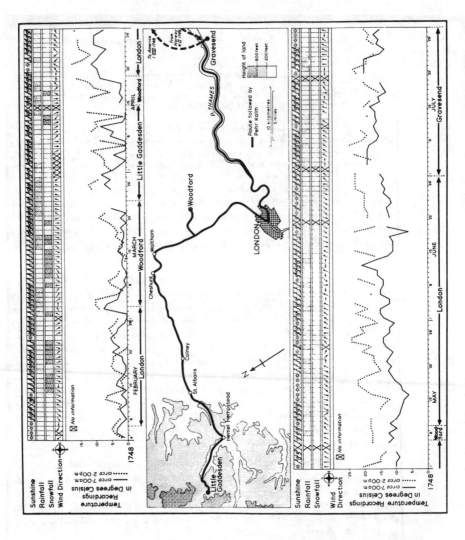

Fig. 4 · Meteorological observations by Pehr Kalm

Throughout his stay in England, Kalm attempted to keep a record of the daily weather conditions – sunshine, rainfall, snow, wind direction and temperatures (according to the scale of his friend Anders Celsius). In this diagram, the observations are set against the background of the places where Kalm stayed. (W.R. Mead, *Historical Geography of Scandinavia*, London, 1983)

Reinhold Forster who was the original translator of the Stockholm version of Kalm's *Travels in North America*. Soon after, the archive of the Linnaean Society in London's Piccadilly not only offered the prospect of some of the North American letters, but also some of the original pressed flowers that he had sent back in them to Uppsala. It was surprising to discover the names of Kalm and his assistant Lars Ljungström listed among the communicants when searching for Finnish names in the early record books of the Swedish church of Ulrika Eleonora. A debt is owed to Carl-Rudolf and Brita Gardberg for regular hospitality in their home by the site of Kalm's original botanical garden on the banks of the Aura river, and to the staff of Piikkiö for demonstrating that, if Kalm's vines succumbed, present-day Canadian stock can flourish at the University's research station. To thumb the rough pages of the dissertations conducted under Kalm's supervision is always a pleasure. They are entertainingly fulsome in their dedications, one even addressed to Sir Pehr Kalm. On another occasion, Carl Skottsberg was so kind as to send a copy of the accounts that Kalm kept so diligently in North America and which he lodged on his return with the Swedish Academy that had supported him. They contain plenty of human touches. There are payments for a French dictionary and an 'English Common Prayer Book', for shoe polish and ink, for brandy when trying to obtain a ship's passage to North America, for beer when he sought to loosen the tongues of Hertfordshire villagers, and for metal shoe buckles (silver ones being too attractive for highwaymen). And for anyone interested in Linnaeus's favourite student, little could be more fascinating than to hold the Åbo copy of the flora that was given to him — *Peresimia botanico floram offert C. Linnaeus* — which Kalm annotated so fully and which bears his monogram on the title page.

By what miracle were six manuscript volumes of the diary preserved? They were presumed destroyed by fire in 1827, but a fair copy was discovered in Helsinki University Library in 1899. Thereafter they remained strangely neglected until Martti Kerkkonen undertook their transcription as a retirement task. Their content is fuller than that of the three volumes published in Stockholm in Kalm's lifetime, for which a different manuscript must have been used.

The text of Kerkkonen's transcription covering Kalm's English journey was received at a difficult personal time. It provided a different kind of

Finnish experience by offering the absorbing task of translating two pages nightly during the many spent on depressing winter train journeys to and from a hospital in Buckinghamshire. Most demanding was the attempt to unscramble the technical details of the agricultural implements that Kalm described and measured with such care during his visit to Little Gaddesden. The translation is unpublished, but the typescript is deposited in the Linnaean collection for whomsoever it may be of interest. Kalm's written language, void of all but simple adjectives and adverbs, reflects the homely character and fidelity of its author. 'My style of writing is very simple', he declared; '[it] will doubtless earn me a low reputation among the nightingales of Pliny'.

A founding father of Finland

It was a summer evening in 1950 at hospitable Bombi and beside the bedside lamp was laid the manuscript diary of Johan Jacob von Julin (1787–1853). It presaged a sleepless night. The diary bore the title *J. Julin Jnr. Notes taken during a journey in Sweden, England, France, Holland, Germany and Denmark. The Years 1815 and 1816*. The English journey runs to 248 pages. In the spring of 1815, Johan Jacob's young wife, sister of Frans Michael Franzén, died. In a letter sent from England, he confessed: 'I sought distraction in a foreign land where new things could absorb the attention of my spirit and dispel grief'. The journey was undertaken in the company of an Åbo friend, Lars von Haartman. It was memorable and productive from the moment of arrival in Harwich Roads on August 19 to July 28, 1816, when he again set foot in Finland. 'Here', he wrote from London, 'everything is so strange and exciting, that I live in a completely new world. It is as if I were not awake but dreamed. I rub my eyes but the dream pictures do not disappear'. Johan Jacob comes alive on many pages of his diary. The exhilaration that he feels on his first stage coach ride comes through, and his zest for living is made evident in a healthy appetite. On St Andrew's Day, it was stimulated by meat pudding and raisin pudding, madeira and port, while a 'mountain Scot' walked up and down playing the bagpipes. Each day was crammed with new experiences: it was a journey of discovery as well as recovery.

There were industrial experiences — breweries, wineries, druggists. Mechanical plants were admired — a shoe factory turning out 300 pairs a day, the steam press that produced 10,000 copies of *The Times* daily, Ardwick mill in Manchester with its 1,400 employees, the division of labour in a Sheffield cutlery works (where Swedish iron was much prized), Birmingham 'the English Nuremberg'. Wedgwood's 'jasper ware' products fascinated him, as did the lustre ware and glazes of Herculaneum pottery. It cheered him to find Åbo deals in the timber yards and amused him to find a statue works. Deptford docks, the West India docks, Liverpool docks all impressed. The environs of Newcastle were alight with foundries — iron, brass and bronze. Technical innovations, small and large, were described — a soda-water machine, Humphry Davy's safety lamp, Westminster Gaslight Company with its 'batswing' burners, the constructional methods of Waterloo and Southwark bridges.

Economic life was represented by visits to the Bank of England, Lloyd's underwriters and the Stock Exchange. Scientific life attracted him to the Royal Society (where Sir Joseph Banks was still active), the Linnaean Society, the Geological Society and the British Museum (where the admired the Elgin Marbles). Social experiences ran the gamut from a deaf and dumb institute to a school for the blind, from Lancaster Bell schools to Sunday schools, from Newgate prison and a Howard Plan prison to Bridewell House of Correction in Edinburgh. Curiosities ranged from the Derbyshire caves to a graphic description of Petticoat Lane. Aesthetic high points were Warwick Castle and the Lake District. As for entertainment, there were pantomimes and performing animals, the royal mantles of Napoleon and Josephine, the Italian opera and productions of The Tempest, Macbeth and Hamlet ('Ophelia, too old'). The winter of 1815–16 was severe and, beside skating on the Serpentine, there was a frost fair on the Thames (John Good, the young sailor from Hull, also described it in his reminiscences). It appears that in some cities, such as Liverpool, there was 'no place of amusement and pleasure'. 'Even the richest bankers [were] at their counters at eleven o'clock in the evening'. However, Liverpool did provide the pleasure of Mr Roscoe's garden (in fact, the very man whose name is commemorated in the Society which occasioned the first personal sortie into Anglo-Finnish relations).

As his base, Johan Jacob used Grove Hall at Bow, east of London, an academy for sixty boys who were called 'parlour boarders' and who paid fifteen guineas a month. It was run by Dr James Lindsay, a Presbyterian Scot hailing from Kirriemuir in Forfarshire. There were four daughters in the family and Johan Jacob returned in 1820 to marry Emilia. At Bombi there are two small oil paintings of Grove Hall, while in Poplar Public Library, there is a charcoal sketch of the house just before it was demolished at the end of the nineteenth century.

The diary was continued in 1820–1 (128 pages) and with diminishing entries in 1825, 1828, 1833 and 1838. In each year, there were extended journeys to different parts of Britain and equally fruitful encounters.

In 1822, Johan Jacob acquired the Fiskars property — 35,000 hectares of land, including iron resources and a modicum of copper. Around it was developed the bruk — a little bit of Swedish Bergslagen beyond the Baltic. It benefited from all the knowledge that he had gained in English and Welsh ironworks, the copper plant of Cornwall and the chemical acumen of France and Sweden. Yrjö Koskelainen subtitled his biographical study of Johan Jacob von Julin 'a pioneer of our industry'. Today, metallurgical and engineering products constitute Finland's principal export by value, and the name Fiskars has an international reputation.

Johan Jacob was equally a pioneer of Finnish agriculture, especially of livestock. His library at Fiskars contained more than 300 English titles, many devoted entirely to the practices and techniques of farming. After spending two days with the diary (and not forgetting the marginal sketches that demonstrated another of its author's attributes), it was equally fascinating to transfer attention to the printed books, annotated with his comments. *Handlingar rörande Finska Landtbruks mötet i Åbo* (1848) yielded up an uncatalogued letter from V. Collin of Mustiala concerning his journey to Scotland to fetch the first Ayrshire cow to Finland in 1848 (Johan Jacob had imported Herefords and Galloways twenty years earlier).

There were social and economic consequences of the journeys which supplemented the industrial and agricultural. Thus, a Lancaster Bell school was established in Åbo according to the English model. It was for Finnish-speaking children and was paid for by the patron himself. He also used British models for the first savings bank to be established in Finland in 1822, while a decade later he was pressing for the establishment of private banks as in Britain and Russia. The motto that he adopted sums up the guiding principles of his busy life: to be industrious, truthful and hopeful — *Toimi, totuus ja toivo*.

Johan Jacob von Julin is buried in Pojo churchyard, but his spirit lives on in the pages of his little-known diaries. His tours parallel in many ways the Swedish study tours gathered together by Sven Rydberg. It is surprising that, unlike those of his brother-in-law, the poet and bishop Frans Michael Franzén, who travelled much of the same territory twenty years earlier, the von Julin diaries have not been published.

Inevitably, there are footnotes to the von Julin episode. Two may be mentioned. First, although the name of Wilkinson is still maintained, commercially speaking, every morning begins with a Fiskars razor blade and is continued in a garden tilled with Fiskars tools. Secondly, there is a

---

Fig. 6 *(opposite)*. A page from the diary of Johan Jacob von Julin

The unpublished diary of Johan Jacob von Julin includes many entries, some accompanied by diagrammatic sketches, about technical inventions and innovations which he observed on his first visit to England in 1815. The extract from the diary refers principally to a dredging machine that attracted Johan Jacob's attention on the banks of the Thames. The Renvall Institute in Helsinki provided a setting for a 1992 reunion with the diary thanks to the kindness of J.-E.L. von Julin, with whose permission the illustration is reproduced.

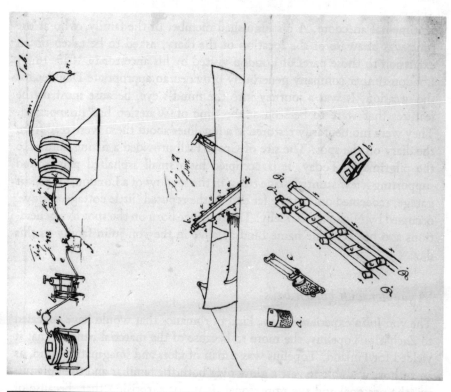

sentimental anecdote. A distinguished member of the family, who at the time was unaware of the location of the diary, asked to be taken on an excursion to those parts of London visited by his ancestor in 1815–16. A London timber company generously provided an appropriate Daimler for the occasion. It was a journey into the mind's eye, because most of the features that were to be seen at the time of Waterloo had disappeared. They were momentarily restored as a few lines about them were read from the diary on the spot. The site of Grove Hall provided a fitting climax to the pilgrimage. Today, it is occupied by a small asphalted playground supporting a few stunted plane trees, in the shadow of a London Transport garage, redeemed only at the far end by the reputed 'little cottage at Bow' occupied by Nicholas Nickleby. The romance born on the spot five generations ago has kept the name Lindsay alive in the von Julin family to this day.

'A juggler with golden balls'

The von Julin experience is the kind of romance that would have appealed to Zacharias Topelius, the more so because of the material benefits that it yielded for Finland. Topelius was a man of ideas and imagination who, as an author, was able to cast a glow over both the familiar and the unfamiliar, the personal and the impersonal. It is not surprising that, because of his prolific output, there is much that is little known. Well-known is his *Boken om vårt land*, which is said to have sold as many copies in his homeland as the Bible. It is a quintessentially Finnish book; so too is *Finland framställdt i teckningar* (1845), the first book of steel engravings of the Finnish landscape, for which he wrote the text. Also well-known are the children's stories, the poems, the hymns, the philosophical essays and (though they may not bear his name) the endless newspaper articles.

Unknown to the outside world, because they have never been translated, are the essays on London. Sailing up the Thames in July 1862, Topelius recorded 'a dark Domesday cloud' over the city — pollution really was pollution in his day. Nelson stood 'black as a powder monkey' on his recently erected column: Wellington's statue was as though he had come 'straight from the field of Waterloo'. Besides dirt, there was noise. In London, wrote Topelius, 'Glamis hath murdered sleep'. The essay on 'The Streets of London', with 'Hogarth-faced crowds' and the pressure of humanity, is outstanding. Topelius subjected himself to the experience of a horse-drawn omnibus — 'a Noah's Ark of a creation', with the passengers 'packed like anchovies'. Minutes, he ruminated, were 'weighed in gold'. Only a 'pane of glass separated riches and poverty'. 'In Paris, this drives men to communism: in London, merely to gin'. The London essays may be read aloud with as much effect as the pages of Charles Dickens

— and have been before an audience of Swedes and Finns at the Swedish church in London, by a professional actor who looked uncannily like Topelius himself. They may be unknown, but at least the London essays are printed.

One substantial contribution by Topelius is virtually unknown because it remains unprinted. For more than a generation, Topelius, as the first professor of Finnish history in the Imperial Alexander University of Helsinki, entertained his students with a regular series of lectures. They were doubtless read from the manuscripts, written in his clear bold script, and presented against the backdrop of Broström's map of Finland which he liked to use. They are full of pregnant observations on the past, present and future of Finland as he saw it, and all are set firmly in their geographical context. They suggest that Topelius was one of the most percipient of Finland's founding fathers. The lectures merit an edited volume in one of Finland's distinguished learned series.

'When you have nothing better to do, read one of those neglected books from the nineteenth century'. The advice of Edgar Kant, the Estonian geographer, might well be applied to the historical lectures of Topelius, who must claim a place in Finnish historiography for a variety of reasons. First, he was a pioneering protagonist of history. He believed that 'a people without a history goes blindfolded down a slippery slope towards an unknown end'. Secondly, none of his predecessors had burrowed so diligently into primary Finnish source materials. In a succession of four lectures, there are references to 32, 25, 59 and 29 sources respectively, independently of scores of references to maps. At the same time, apart from limited reference to Scandinavian literature, Topelius often echoed the thinking of his European contemporaries without appearing to know of their work. The publications of the German pedagogue Carl Ritter are representative. The borrower's book of the University Library in Helsinki records what Topelius took out while giving his lecture series. Thirdly, Topelius sought to breathe life into history, not to 'dissect it as in an anatomy chamber'. Partly in this context, he believed that everyday things had a place in history as well as great events. Thus, the introduction of fruit and vegetable seeds to Finland as well as of domestic animals found a place in his story. Fourthly, history was employed by Topelius to look forward as well as backward. He forecast a time when Finland would be capable of supporting seven million inhabitants (it had only a million and a half in his day). At the same time, in his springtime lectures of 1866, he was fearful of the prospective social tensions that a concentration of wealth in a few hands might engender — the pending conflict of capitalism and communism, as he called it, 'capable of involving the whole of European society'. He was also an early protagonist of neutrality — ideally of a neutral Finland in a neutral Baltic Sea.

It is not difficult to criticise Topelius as an historian. He was writing before specialists divided the study of history into periods and refined it into sub-disciplines. There is a strong determinist streak in his interpretation of events. History also had lessons to teach and there is an element of moral posturing in his work. In addition, he was a born romantic. For him, history had something of the quality of an historical novel. There are certainly pages in the lectures that recall his *Surgeon's Tales*. Stylistically, there are features that impair his work — the parable is introduced too often for modern taste. Yet his sharp observations, epigrams and metaphors give a persistent vitality to his work. Was he the first to write that 'the freedom that most political people strive after is the freedom to bind others in chains'?

More than a century has passed since the death of Topelius. His last home in Hertonäs, now swallowed up in suburban Helsinki, is less than the shrine that it might be. How pleasant if the windows could be labelled with the names that he gave them. For him, they were 'magic casements' such as the poet John Keats dreamed of. Topelius endowed each of them with its appropriate heavenly name — Aurora, the window to the east, Betelguse, the big window; Venus, the window admitting the evening star. It was the octogenarian displaying a marvellously childlike quality. This imagination, together with his natural fluency enabled him to combine the roles of scholar and columnist, pedagogue and poet, novelist and moralist. To be acquainted with his work is to recall a phrase coined by Max Beerbohm. In so many ways, Zacharias Topelius was 'a juggler with golden balls'.

Geographical pioneering

'Are the golden flowers still shining on the hills of Altai. Is the pale moon still shining on the hills of the golden mountains?' It is not Topelius this time, but two lines from a nuptial song on which Johannes Gabriel Granö meditated in the 'great sanctuary of flowers' that he encountered during his years of travel in the Altai.

'Yes, yes', was the answer, 'the alpine meadows still dress themselves in the golden brilliance of their flowers . . . The yellow alpine poppies nod on the edge of the springs, the alpine buttercups open their shining blooms on the soft carpets of moss, the violets follow the movements of the sun in the sky'.

In 1947, Johannes Granö was kind enough to arrange a meeting with one who did not really know much about him at the old geographical institute in Hakaniemi. In a shadowy room and in quietly spoken French, he talked of his work and philosophy. Only much later did the character of his geographical contribution make an impact.

First, there was the fascination of his upbringing and the consequences that it obviously had for his personal and academic development. His childhood was spent in Omsk, where his father was appointed by the Lutheran church to minister to the spiritual needs of the Finnish immigrant community as well as to the Finnish political dissidents who had been banished to the area and who constituted a virtual university in exile. While for many the immense and little-known territories of interior Russia were an incubus, for Granö they proved a stimulus. In 1905, he wrote about the Finnish colonies in Siberia (there was even one called Helsinki), before proceeding on a succession of expeditions to Mongolia, Tienshan and Amur, supported by the Finno-Ugrian Society. There followed in 1913–16 a series of investigations on the geomorphology and glaciology of the Altai, advancing the work of earlier Russian scholars whose publications are for the most part either unknown or forgotten.

Secondly, behind and beyond the theories that Granö conceived concerning the evolution of these hitherto unexplored territories, there was the originality of the methodology employed in his field studies and the tenacity with which he pursued them. The landscape profiles from Uranchai and northern Mongolia as well as the varied and detailed diagrams from Altai reflect his imagination and ingenuity. They represent the scientific measurement and assessment of the physical world that complement the subjective impressions of some 10,000 kilometres of travel.

But the principal interest in his work has been generated by *Puhdas maantiede*, commonly translated as 'Pure geography', published in 1930 and a study unique for its time. Its originality lay in its treatment of and attitude to sensory experiences — in particular the representation of visual reactions to the landscape. Taking the island of Valosaari as his experimental territory, Granö gave cartographic expression to the contrast between the physical space as presented by the scientist and the self-conceived space of the ordinary observer — the sights, sounds, colours, seasonal changes, the near and the far. There was an immediate German translation, but sixty years were to pass before a competent English translation began to seek a publisher.

And a turbulent century was to pass before the descendants of the Finnish colonists in and around Omsk were to be sought out by visitors from Finnish Radio. The colony of Helsinki may have disappeared, but they found the Lutheran parsonage still standing, occupied by three Russian families, and awaiting a visit from the grandson of its first occupant.

While fate carried Johannes Granö to the Eurasian heartland, choice took his friend Väinö Auer to Patagonia. He is remembered personally as a vivacious octogenarian, loquacious about Topelius, a sparkle in his eye and a crackle in his throaty voice. Between 1928 and 1954, Väinö Auer conducted thirteen expeditions to Tierra del Fuego (Tulimaa to Finns),

constructing a complete chronology of its Quaternary geomorphology and
at one time having as many a forty young Argentinians as his assistants.
His widespread employment of pollen analysis and production of peatland
profiles probably constituted the largest project of its kind down to his
time. There may be no companion volume of travels comparable to that of
Granö in the Altai, but compensatingly there is a fine acknowledgement
of the scientific value of his investigations in a report to the *Proceedings of
the Royal Society of London*. Two generations later, his example has stimulated a new generation of Finns, equipped with new information and new
techniques, to follow in his tracks and extend his enquiries.

In general, the contributions of Finns to geographical discovery has
received scant international attention. A corrective has been supplied by
Matka-arkku (The Traveller's Chest), a review of Finnish exploration and
journeyings. It covers Finnish endeavours from the Arctic to the Tropics,
from the Arab World to China, and especially in the broad wastes of the
old Russian Empire — from Kola to Kamchatka and Alaska. *Matka-arkku*
received an award as the best scientific publication of its year. It remains
another of those books closed to the rest of the world by language.

A past worthy of the present

Over the last two generations, history has become a virtual industry in
Finland, for history serves a national function. It certainly makes a sizeable
contribution to the flood of academic publications that a seemingly hyper-
active university community offers to the public. Its principal sources are
documentary and, as Finland has become more affluent, it has been possible to invest more time and energy into their collection and preservation.
The first archives to claim attention were those of ecclesiastical, legal,
constitutional and political consequence. They had a home built for them
— *Valtionarkisto*, the National Archives — on a rocky outcrop in central
Helsinki, midway between the ornate House of the Estates and the Bank of
Finland.

Somewhat differently from other countries, Finland has treasured
another collection of archival material for which fine accommodation was
built a century ago by the fifty-year-old Finnish Literary Society.
Hallituskatu Number One symbolises the status of ethnographic studies in
Finland. For anyone interested in folk poetry alone, it is exciting to have
touched some of the original pages of Elias Lönnrot's *Kalevala* material
and to have been in the presence of the million and a quarter lines of orally
transmitted verse that makes the building something of a Finnish shrine.
Again, for students interested in field studies, it is appealing to find among
the Society's collections, notebooks such as those kept by a group of
youthful enthusiasts who called themselves *Muurahaiset*, the Ants (did

they know that Francis Bacon likened empiricists to ants?). The notebooks of *Muurahaiset* provided a model for a generation of fieldworkers. *Muurahaiset* were, in fact, following in the tradition of Lönnrot and Castrén — and of the less-known A.J. Sjögren, whose diaries and field notes, *Ephmerider* (1806–55), extend over much of his lifetime and which have been the subject of pioneering work by Michael Branch.

There are memories of devoted custodians of such collections — of Eric Holmberg patiently editing the Porthan papers at Åbo Akademi, of Martti Kerkkonen meticulously transcribing the eighteenth-century script of Pehr Kalm's diaries, of Jorma Vallinkoski attempting to piece together the charred fragments of the record books of Åbo Akademi rescued from the fire in 1827. It has been comforting to know that at least some of the generation of retired custodians who in their day laboured with such limited resources have lived to see their prized collections receiving the care and attention they deserve.

An outstanding example of the revaluation of a national treasure is provided by the library and map collection of Adolf Erik Nordenskiöld. For too long after its far-sighted acquisition from Sweden, this collection — which is of European stature — was crowded into the topmost storey of the University Library, to the despair of its devoted curator Anne-Marie Mickwitz. Today, thanks to the initiative of Esko Häkli, it is catalogued in no less than four quarto volumes, enjoys an impressive display room and is a place of pilgrimage, especially for cartographers, from all over the world.

Together with other examples, the rehabilitation of the Nordenskiöld collection has not been without consequences elsewhere. To take a precise example, it was clear that the neglected archive of the Royal Geographical Society of London (of which Nordenskiöld himself was a gold medallist) contained materials of considerably greater consequence than some which had received handsome treatment in Finland. In the process of cataloguing, the archive yielded its own handful of Finnish materials. Thus, the correspondence of Finland's first Arabist, Georg August Wallin, with the Society's secretary came to light. Much more exciting, the manuscripts of his journeys through Arabia in 1846, which he has sent for publication in the *Geographical Journal*, literally slipped out of the open-ended envelopes in which they had been casually returned from the printer in 1848. In fact, Georg August Wallin — a less colourful but no less qualified Arabist than Richard Burton — had preceded Burton on a pilgrimage to Mecca.

The London experience is happily complemented by that of Kaj Öhrnberg in St Petersburg, where he has brought to light Wallin papers which had remained untouched for the greater part of a century and a half. As with the minor treasure-trove of Sjögren papers uncovered there by Michael Branch, they offer examples of the significance of the academic community of the old Russian capital for nineteenth-century Finnish scientists and men of letters.

The distinctiveness of Finnish history emerges because of and in spite of the histories of neighbouring Sweden and Russia. In the past, there have been accepted interpretations and 'official' versions of events, with history appearing to sanction — even to sanctify — actions. Hitherto, most Finnish history has been published in Finnish for readers in the homeland. With the regular use of one of the world languages by Finnish historians, their publications are increasingly widely circulated. The consequent incorporation of aspects of Finland's history into world history imparts a new authority not only to Finnish historians, but to Finland itself.

Behind history is geography, a subject which in the course of two generations has acquired a new status in Finnish universities. It has been exciting to witness the blossoming of the century-old research series *Fennia*, the transformation of the journal *Terra* and the reputation that geographers have acquired across a broad spectrum of the arts and sciences — and, as with so much academic endeavour in Finland, to see the results commanding international attention.

5

THE RECORD OF THE LAND AND ITS PEOPLE

'I am prepared to gamble that in 24 hours I could teach an intel-
ligent *bonde* who can neither read nor write the way to draw a
general map.' (O.F. Wetterhof, 'Militarisk Beskrifning öfver
Svenska Carelen samt tankar om dess Förswar',
MS. *c*. 1780, Krigsarkivet, Stockholm, p. 33)

Innovations in documentation

Anyone interested in the geography of Finland rapidly encounters its maps
and censuses — and soon appreciates that, in parallel with those of
Sweden, they are of exceptional quality and unusual antecedence. From
these two sources can be gleaned facts and figures that tell of the advance
and retreat of settlement as well as of the effects of disease, famine and war
as the Horsemen of the Apocalypse rode all too frequently across the land.
The gleanings will be scantier than for much of Western Europe before
1600, though the *Atlas of the Settlement in Finland in the late 1560s*, based on
the cadastres (*jordeböcker*) of landed property and painstakingly assembled
by Eino Jutikkala and his colleagues, offers an exceptional comment.

From a personal standpoint, there have been three points of departure
— the foundation of *Lantmäteristyrelsen* in Stockholm in 1627; the
establishment of *Tabellverket*, the Tables of Mortality, in 1749; and
storskiftet, the land reorganisation legislation which was initiated simultaneously. *Tabellverket* called for a regular documentation of the people,
which enabled forecasts about future developments as well as contemporary assessment. Behind the land reorganisation programme lay generations of experience in territorial survey, in detailed identification of taxable
features, and in the acquisition and employment of surveying equipment.
Tabellverket and *storskiftet* in combination set in motion a record unique for
its time.

A third agency, little known outside Finland, may be fittingly considered in their company, although its operation was by comparison modest
both in time and scope. In 1797, an organisation independent of the state
was formed to promote the economic development of the Grand Duchy.
It was *Finska Hushållningssällskapet*, the Finnish Economic Society.
Through its members, new techniques and new ideas were widely propagated, and the first economic surveys of Finland were conducted. Its papers
were long a neglected source of historical information.

The mapping of the land

The first historic map covering Finland to make a personal impact was the *Carta marina* of Olaus Magnus, a woodcut produced in Venice in 1539. It disappeared some time during the 1570s and was rediscovered in Munich in 1886. For no other part of the world from the time is there a pictorial map of such quality as that which Olaus Magnus prepared for the Scandinavian world. It holds up a mirror to Finland and is a continual source of enlightenment and entertainment. Together with his *Historia de gentibus septentrionalibus* which was published for Olaus Magnus in Rome in 1555, it has provided vignettes to set many aspects of Finnish life in perspective. The mounted skirmishes on the Finnish Gulf against the Muscovites and the features of ice-clad Viipuri lent themselves to reproduction during the Winter War of 1939–40. It is a reflection of the changed value of antiquarian books that in 1939 the English translation of *de gentibus* (printed in London in 1658) could still be bought for about the same price as a facsimile of the *Carta marina* printed by the University Library in Uppsala thirty years later.

With the disappearance of the *Carta marina* the outside world had to await the contributions of seventeenth-century Swedish mapmakers before the cartographic features of Finland were more accurately delineated and widely disseminated. Long before he was appointed director of *Lantmäteristyrelsen*, Anders Bure worked with his cousin on the preparation of a map of northern Scandinavia (including Finland and Kola), which for the first time showed the disputed boundary between the Swedish and Danish realms. In 1626 he published the copper plate *Orbis arctoi nova et accurata* which became the definitive statement of its time and determined for a long time the representation of the Nordic lands on the map of Europe. Interest in Bure's map was to mark the beginning of an attempt to unravel, in collaboration with Stig Jaatinen, the historical representation of the Grand Duchy in old British maps and atlases.

Personally, it was also a revelation to find that some of the earliest large-scale maps of Finland (1:5,000–1:15,000) were being made less than a decade after the establishment of *Lantmäteristyrelsen*. Anders Strengh drew and coloured his maps of Naapila and Rajalahti hamlets in Orivesi parish as early as 1634. 'First start with a compass rose,' ran an early

---

Fig. 7 *(opposite)*. A hamlet in Sund, Åland, from a late seventeenth-century chartbook

The Land Survey Office of Finland has a collection of historic maps of Finland, including several volumes of taxation maps from the late seventeenth century. The taxed features of the cluster of farmsteads that make up the hamlet are identified on the left hand side of the map. (Courtesy, Maanmittaushallitus, Helsinki)

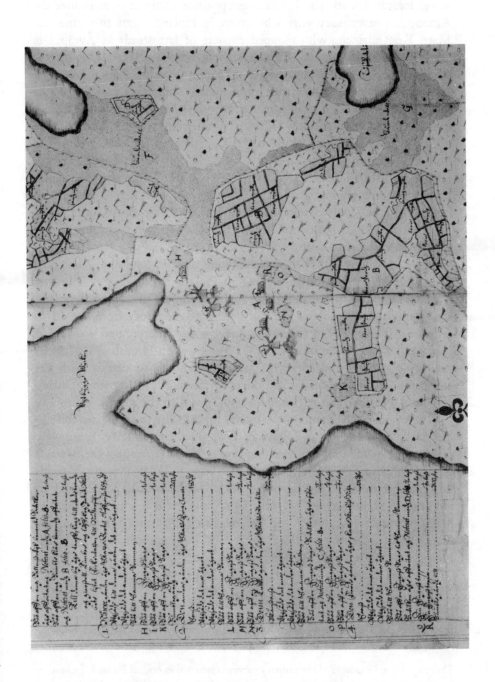

instruction to surveyors — and the maps from Pälkäne and Kangasala were decorated with the handsomest possible compass embellishments. Among the seven surveyors who arrive in Finland about this time was Matti Ruotsalainen, who mapped clusters of farmsteads in Äyräpää in the Karelian peninsula, and Hans Hansson, who was responsible for the taxation map of Haraldsby in Åland (1650). Volumes containing their maps and other cadastral maps, once housed somewhat casually in the archive room of the old *Lantmäteristyrelsen/Maanmittaushallitus* headquarters in Helsinki, are now treasured as museum items.

The rich survey material from the Land Survey Office has remained little known abroad, although both in Sweden and Finland its history has been recorded in substantial anniversary volumes. To be properly appreciated, the cartographic products of *Lantmäteristyrelsen* have to be placed in their international context. Methodologically, they display unique features anticipating, for example, much that has generally been regarded as original in eighteenth-century French cartography.

Not surprisingly, other than the taxation motive, the impulse behind a great deal of the early map-making in Finland was military. The first material produced in Finland itself touched upon the eastern border country. Jaakko Teitti's sketch-plans of part of the territory from the 1570s remained largely forgotton until they were incorporated in Kyösti Julku's doctoral dissertation in 1987. The Swedish-Finnish army had its military engineers and surveyors who were much concerned with the construction of fortifications and the preparation of military sites. During the Great Northern War (*Isoviha/Stora Ofreden* to the Finns), officers of the survey corps were among the troops captured by the Russians following the Swedish defeat at Poltava in 1709. In their captivity, some were dispatched to undertake pioneer surveys in Siberia. Among them was a Finn, C.G. Granfelt. After the Peace of Nystad in 1721, he returned to his homeland. His diary, on display at Turku castle, is unforgettable for its last poignant sentence — '*Til Åbo i Jesu Namn*'. It is strange to think that he may have contributed to the early eighteenth-century Swedish survey maps of Siberia rediscovered in St Petersburg by August Strindberg during his early days as a university librarian.

At least Granfelt returned. Other Finns whose fate in Swedish

---

Fig. 8 *(opposite)*. A part of Jorois/Joroinen surveyed by *Finska Recognoserings-verket, c.* 1775

The map, a good example of the military survey conducted in central Finland, focuses on the estate of Frugård (conjuring up memories of a horse-drawn landau, waiting at the station, which Sven-Erik Åström drove to what was a summer idyll). (Courtesy *Krigsarkivet*, Stockholm)

settlements and buildings and was not a wilderness of trees, rocks and log cabins. The inclusion of Finland's castles and coats-of-arms accorded to the Grand Duchy at least a touch of grandeur.

Already by the time that *Recognoseringsverket* was under way, a generation of land-surveyors had been working on maps to accompany the reorganisation of rural properties. The *storskifte (isojako)* law of 1749 authorised the majority of landowners in a community to apply for the compacting of their scattered holdings into consolidated units. Principally because the *Storskifte* documents were the basis for tax assessments, they have been husbanded in Finland with a care which contrasts with the fate that befell most maps accompanying the equivalent British Parliamentary Enclosure awards. Land reorganisation has been repeated at a number of intervals through subsequent legislation. As a result, there is a record of Finnish land-use changes which, in some cases, covers more than two centuries. For anyone interested in the cadastral systems of western Europe, Finnish (and Swedish) documentation is remarkable, not least because it preceded the compilations of the French *cadastres*. Finnish interest in the historico-geographical potentialities of *storskifte* material, mostly on a scale of 1:4,000, was slow to develop. Michael Jones has used it to trace the social and legal consequences of land emergence along the Ostrobothnian coast, while the same source has been employed by Stig Jaatinen and his colleagues to construct an impressive map of the eighteenth-century cultural landscape of the Åland islands.

Labouring with these topographical and cadastral materials and by dint of much scissors-and-paste work, the 'amiable and accomplished' C.F. af Hällström (as Edward Clarke called him) compiled the first *Atlas of Finland* (1799). It was published as the second volume of the *Atlas of Sweden* and appeared under the name of S.G. Hermelin — his name remains attached to the mass of working materials in the files of the Swedish Military Archive. The *Atlas of Finland* contained six maps, with an engraving of the Häme landscape as a frontispiece. The good fortune of purchasing an unbound copy of the *Atlas* from an antiquarian bookseller at a modest price recalled an unexpected night's shelter on the Hällström estate in Ostrobothnia some twenty years earlier.

Simultaneously with *Recognoseringsverket*, attention was directed to the need for a reliable hydrographic survey. The early 'waggoners' or 'mariners mirrors' printed by Dutch and British hydrographers in the seventeenth century were of little practical value for navigators in Finnish waters. It was left to the energies of Admiral af Klercker to supervise a detailed survey of the critical channels round the coast of Finland. From row-boats in summer and through ice holes in winter, plumb-lines were dropped and the slow, meticulous plotting of navigable channels proceeded. The patience required for the task can be imagined from the autobiographical notes of A.G.af Schultén (in Åbo Akademi) and from a glimpse of the fading transparencies of the working papers first seen in the family chest of the af Schultén-Lownertz family, and later in the archive of the Akademi. More accurate charts of the south-western archipelagos were slowly produced from the 1770s onwards.

Side by side with the compilation of the *Atlas of Sweden/Finland* and under the supervision of Admiral Nordenanker the compilation of the first large maritime atlas of the Baltic proceeded under the name of Gustaf af Klint. But, comprehensively though the territorial waters of Finland might be presented, no chart could dispense with the trained eye of the pilot.

It was comforting to encounter the first echo-sounding devices when travelling on the swift naval patrol vessels in the Åland archipelago (and fascinating to be able to appreciate the unusually fiord-like profiles of the north shore inlets, profiles which appear to await a glaciological explanation). Less wary summer yachtsmen leave the marked sea-lanes at their peril — though to the advantage of local repair yards.

Finland has appeared on the map of Europe for 500 years. Map-making in Finland would not have aroused the same personal interest had not the late Brian Harley commissioned chapters on the Nordic Countries for the *World History of Cartography* that is being published by the Chicago University Press. There are memories of an early visit to see the collection of Carl Enckell, now available on video disc. Beyond the scope of the *World History*, much pleasure has been derived from the remarkable collection of thematic maps of Finland, especially from the nineteenth century, assembled by Sakari Härö.

The record of the people

Finnish churches are generally locked except during the hours of divine service. On weekdays their registry offices, now often modern extensions to vicarages and operated by sociable civil servants, have offered a haven in inclement weather and a harvest of potential footnotes on what might otherwise have been an unrewarding day. There are memories of retreating to the church registries of Iisalmi, Nurmes, Kuusamo, Joroinen and Saltvik. The principal attraction has been the legacy of *Tabellverket*, the tables of mortality, the maintenance of which was an obligation placed on the clergy in every parish.

It is not generally appreciated that Sweden was the first country to initiate a nationwide and continuous collection of vital statistics. As a Grand Duchy and integral part of Sweden, Finland has accordingly inherited a similarly long and detailed record of its people. Births, marriages and deaths had been recorded by the clergy since the latter part of the seventeenth century, but after 1748 printed proformas were provided, one for the central record, one to be retained by the parish. From 1752 onwards at triennial intervals and from 1775, with a modified formula, at quinquennial intervals a return was required of the age, status and employment of all inhabitants. When Finland became a Grand Duchy of Russia in 1809 and the earlier territories of the south-east were restored in 1812, *Tabellverket* continued and was extended to them.

In 1751, the population of Finland was estimated as 429,912. The census of 1805, shortly before the loss of the Grand Duchy to Russia, provided a figure of 898,364. From the outset, the categories into which the population was divided caused problems of identification for the clergy. In 1790, no less than fifty-eight categories of employment were listed on the forms: the military alone accounted for eight. The old were divided into those able to work and those unable to work. There were the halt, blind, deaf and dumb to be singled out no less than the saltpetre workers and the pearl fishers. There was even a column for artists — about thirty were identified, some listed as under fifteen. There was a nil return for architects.

The need for the collection of vital statistics of this kind was prompted by several facts. With pressure from Russia and the constant threat of war, it was necessary to know something about the actual and potential recruitment of able-bodied men for military purposes and where they were resident. It was also important to be able to estimate food requirements, since many parts of the country were subject to famine. The pages of *Tabellverket* always provided a space for observations on the harvest. By the turn of the century, agricultural returns were set beside the demographic; they included the numbers of farm animals (including pairs of oxen, together with the number of *tunnland* sown in relation to them) and the average yield of different crops on the sown part of the cultivated land expressed in terms of crop increase over seed sown.

West European countries long remained unfamiliar with *Tabellverkett*. It was not reported by a British observer until more than half a century after its introduction. Thomas Thomson, a perceptive Scottish geologist and erstwhile author of a history of the Royal Society, included references to it in the Appendix to his *Travels in Sweden during the autumn of 1812* (1813). He was particularly interested in the agricultural returns — 'one of the most curious agricultural documents ever founded by any country'. He recommeded them to the attention of the British Board of Agriculture. It is strange that *Tabellverket* claimed so little attention from Thomas Malthus who, subsequent to his travels in Scandinavia in 1799–1800, published a succession of revisions of his celebrated *Essay on Population*. For comparative purposes it is worth noting that the first British census was conducted in 1801 and that the first attempt to produce comparative information on crop returns, conducted largely through the country clergy, began in 1805.

The first personal acquaintance with church registers was made in the later 1940s at Kuusamo, where the vicar offered shelter from a snowstorm. Kuusamo's late eighteenth-century records made a lasting impression because they identified the waves of epidemics (sometimes noted as originating beyond the border) that afflicted the pioneer community. There were also references to incursions by marauding Russians and wild animals. The church records of Nurmes were found to repeat the saga of epidemics — smallpox and measles in 1754, 1763 and 1771; scarlet fever in 1777, 1783 and 1791. The register of Saltvik congregation, the office of which provided a retreat from summer rain, had a continuity superior to that of many churches. They also included excellent in- and out-migration statistics for the parish from 1805 to 1843.

One of the saddest chapelries visited was that of Seili in the Åbo archipelago, although its records are no longer available on the spot. A leper colony was established at Seili in the eighteenth century and the afflicted community built its own substantial timber church. Seili recalls Peter Richards and the chapter on Finland in his study of *The Medieval Leper and his Northern Heirs* (1977). At Seili, one tragic community succeeded another. With the elimination of leprosy, the hospital became a retreat for the mentally deranged. The hospital building is now a research institute of the University of Turku. As a record of its earlier history, a macabre cell has been retained in its original form. Its extraordinary black-and-white chequerboard walls reflect the curative theory of some early psychiatric practitioner. The contrast with the idyllic natural world beyond is impossible to convey.

The materials resulting from two-and-a-half centuries of population recording in Finland are a demographer's delight. In Sweden a population database has been established at the University of Umeå, with a view to computerising the mass of information arising from *Tabellverket* and related records. It is the ultimate exercise in 'political arithmetic', as the science was once called. There is no technical reason why it could not be repeated in Finland.

Among the many clerical headaches resulting from *Tabellverket* in earlier times, those defining causes of death must have been the worst; no less than thirty causes were tabulated in the first proformas. Medical practitioners were unavailable at that time over most of Finland, and even at the end of the eighteenth century only a score were listed, all but two of these being in the towns. It is a far cry from the contemporary medico-statistical scene. Given the tradition of record-keeping, manageable population numbers and the country's relatively isolated location, Finland is in some respects a natural laboratory for medical statisticians. That it should be one of the few countries where every positive case of HIV-I is reported to the National Board of Health is additionally a reflection of mental attitudes. Scientists have not been slow to construct a diffusion model from which the spread of the disease can be forecast.

A survey of the economy

By the end of the eighteenth century the cartographic surveys of Finland were well established and the returns from *Tabellverket* had been made for two generations. Under the rectorship of Henrik Gabriel Porthan, Åbo Akademi had emerged as an intellectual centre of some renown. But as yet there had been only limited surveys of the Finnish economy. True, there were the reports from the provincial governors (*Landshövdingarnas berättelser*), as well as some exceptional investigations such as the mineralogical report of Daniel Tilas. Porthan himself encouraged the preparation of parish descriptions — topographical accounts of the kind that were being produced in Denmark and Sweden. He also wrote the first geography of his homeland — *Geographie öfver Storfurstendömet Finland* (1795). Strangely, it fails to pay attention to either *Lantmäteristyrelsen* or *Tabellverket*.

In university circles at Åbo a number of societies had come into being, but none was directly concerned with promoting the Finnish economy. Although models existed in Denmark and Sweden, it was to the British Board of Agriculture that attention was directed when it was decided to found the Finnish Economic Society (*Finska Hushållningssällskapet*) in 1797. The Society came into being on the initiative of a small group of friends who were of the physiocratic persuasion. Their objectives were to gather information about the general economic situation and to take practical steps to improve it. Since the Finnish economy was based almost entirely on the exploitation of primary resources, attention was focused on cropping and stocking, husbandry methods and handicrafts. Not least because it had been largely neglected, *Finska Hushållningssällskapets* archive, once it had been given some semblance of order, could not fail to attract attention. It became a personal obsession.

Membership of the Society rose rapidly to a stable 400. Most members lived in south-west Finland, although there was a scattering of enthusiasts in the backwoods of the interior as well as in the outermost parishes of Åland. Membership consisted of administrators, larger landowners, military officers and, above all, clergy. The clergy had mostly studied at Åbo Akademi, were usually known to each other, often had their own church farms (which were not infrequently centres of diffusion of ideas) and were accustomed to playing a pastoral role in their communities. In some respects they were the critical element in the network of membership.

A secretariat was established, the proceedings of its meetings were published, and almost immediately it found itself responsible for supervising a number of projects important for the material improvement of Finnish rural life.

On the left bank of the Aura river in Åbo, there is a handsome Empire-style house bearing the motif of a sword and ploughshare, which has escaped the destruction suffered by neighbouring buildings. It once housed the substantial and long uncatalogued archives of *Finska Hushållningssällskapet*. The fire risk of the building was considerable, and its structural hazards were not to be disregarded — the heavily ornamented ceiling moulding and the central chandelier in the first floor salon once collapsed over a table on which manuscripts had been left overnight. Safe custody has been guaranteed by the transfer of the Society's collection to the security of Åbo Akademi library where, as a labour of love, Lars Zilliacus has compiled a series of descriptive catalogues of the contents of the early volumes.

The first officers of the Society who kept the record-books were honorary and all held other appointments. Their ideas rapidly involved them in what must have been a ferment of activity. They sought reports for publication. They set in motion a series of prize essays similar to those of the British Board of Agriculture, though with rather more formidable titles. Topics assumed a considerable degree of literacy among competitors — *Omne utile laudandum, Viljan är halfva verket, Dulce et decorum est pro patria mori*. Some submissions, including a highly informative statement on the Ostrobothnian economy, came independently and anonymously. Members were also encouraged to make recommendations for the award of medals to *bonder* known to them for their conspicuous enterprise in land reclamation, ditching, stone walling, farm building construction and handicrafts.

Improved farming equipment was encouraged by the establishment in Åbo of a workshop, with a *mechanicus practicus* where model ploughs and other implements from Sweden, Denmark and Britain were displayed. ('The plough was rude and clumsy, the sickle as old as Tubal Cain . . . the flail was unchanged since the Aryan exodus' — Henry Adams's words

Fig. 9 *(opposite)*. Maps prepared from the Statistical Collection of Carl Christian Böcker

During the early 1820s, Carl Christian Böcker gathered together for the first time from most of the parishes of Finland some eighty items of information. The centres that provided returns for his census are identified on the top left hand map. The three other maps illustrate the distribution of precise features listed in the statistical returns. (W.R. Mead, in *Näkökulmia menneisyyteen, Eino Jutikkalan Juhlakirja*, Helsinki, 1967)

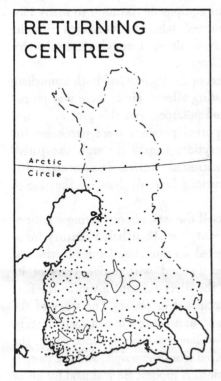

RETURNING
CENTRES

Arctic
Circle

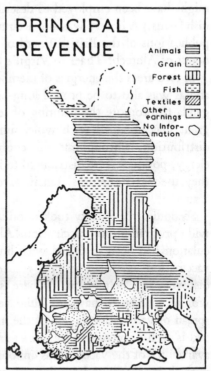

PRINCIPAL
REVENUE

Animals
Grain
Forest
Fish
Textiles
Other
earnings
No Infor-
mation

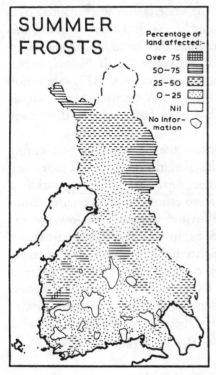

SUMMER
FROSTS

Percentage of
land affected:-

Over 75
50–75
25–50
0–25
Nil
No Infor-
mation

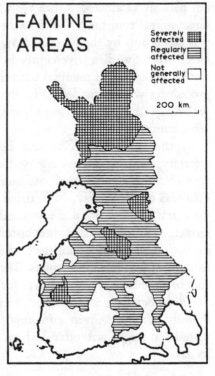

FAMINE
AREAS

Severely
affected
Regularly
affected
Not
generally
affected

200 km.

might have been employed to describe equipment common to many Finnish farms.) A library was also accumulated, where books ranged from the publications of the British Board of Agriculture, through the husbandry books of Albrecht Thaer to Virgil's *Georgics*.

In two areas the energies of members of the Society had both immediate and as was also to be proved long-lasting effects. First, there was propaganda to promote the planting of seed potatoes. For this project a royal grant was obtained with which imported potatoes were purchased for distribution. Throughout the countryside, largely through the parish clergy, potatoes were distributed to interested farmers. The *bomarken* that they used as signatures remain as curious hieroglyphics on the receipt forms.

Secondly, the Society took upon itself the task of conducting a nationwide programme of vaccination. Already for about half-a-century innoculation had been practised with limited success. The Jenner method of vaccination against smallpox reached Finland within five years of its discovery in Cheltenham. (Where is the silver pendant given to the first woman in Åbo to have her child vaccinated in 1802?) The story of the spread of vaccination is one of the most unusual in Finnish social history and is well-documented by *Finska Hushållningssällskapet*. Once again, the availability of the vaccine was announced from the pulpit, and the clergy, with their cantors undertook vaccination. A modest fee was paid for every ten persons vaccinated. Once again, the undertaking was financed by a direct grant from the Swedish exchequer. As with the potato grant, this was taken over by the Russian crown when the Grand Duchy was transferred from Swedish sovereignty in 1809. When *Gamla Finland*, southeastern Finland, was reunited with the Grand Duchy in 1812, vaccination procedures were extended to it. By 1820 it was estimated that a higher percentage of the Finnish population had been vaccinated than that of any other country.

By that time Carl Christian Böcker, the Society's longest-serving secretary, was experimenting with his inquiries into the character and resources of Finland's rural communities. Again, with the cooperation of members of the Society, he initiated a succession of questionnaires. Some were restricted to local areas; some invited selected estate-owners and farmers to keep records of their operations. In the early 1820s there was set in motion an enquiry consisting of eighty items. Returns were obtained from most parishes and hamlets. Their contents are not precisely comparable because they are not always for the same year. Nevertheless *Böckers Statistiska Samling*, as it is called, amounts to the first statistical review of Finnish farming. Given contemporary methods of handling statistical material, it might well offer the basis for an atlas of agricultural activity for its day.

The fire in Åbo in 1827 is presumed to have destroyed some of Böcker's materials. In any case, a decline in Böcker's energies made him realise that he would be unable to fulfil his ambition of producing a complete statistical survey of Finland. The page after page of his mathematical scribblings testify to the feverish energy that he put into the project before he wrote to Nicholas I, in the diplomatic French of the day, that he must relinquish his endeavour. 'Day by day the task proves too difficult for one man'.

The archive of *Finska Hushållningssällskapet* accounts for many rewarding hours spent in the welcoming library of Åbo Akademi, the bells of the cathedral chiming time away all too quickly. Local historians are indebted to the archive for many a paragraph in the stories of their parishes — parishes in which there are still features which bear witness to the activities of a Society which sought to bring into being a Finland that was more than a silhouette of itself.

Omne utile laudandum

Old maps, old seacharts, *Tabellverket*, *Finska Hushållningssällskapet* — all had their uses in their own day. All, through their revaluation by present-day scholars, have opened new windows on Finland's past. All have their modern counterparts.

The presses of *Maanmittaushallitus* in the high-rise office complex in Pasila produce maps with a technical skill second to none. To have witnessed the advance from ground survey, through air photography (with aerial survey developing into an export industry in its own right), through photogrammetry (to which Finland has made its own innovative contributions) to the employment of satellite information for mapping is to have seen the transformation of yet another sector of the Finnish economy. In the process, Finland has been discovered from outer space — by night as well as by day, because the intensity and distribution of radiated artificial light offer a new measure of activity and wealth.

Simultaneously, Finnish-made computers, enjoying a world market, digest what Jörn Donner has called the 'cathedral-like towers of figures' produced by a Central Statistical Office of which Gabriel Rein first took charge in 1865. Sweden bestowed on Finland a concern for facts and figures. The statistical inheritance has enabled geographers to compile their distribution maps — statistical landscapes. It has also fostered a new generation of futurologists and theorists whose manipulative abilities are as ingenious and whose appetites for statistics are as insatiable as those anywhere in the world.

The information revolution has sprung out of such early strivings as those conducted by the members of the Finnish Economic Society. The reports of self-generating government commissions and committees are the present-day equivalents of their early surveys and enquiries. Eye-catching colours may have replaced the undistinguished brown and buff covers that enclosed them, but they have done nothing to halt the increasing speed of obsolescence which consigns them with alarming haste to the crowded shelves of library storerooms.

6

LIVING SPACE AND WORKING PLACE

'... more space where nobody is than where somebody is'
(Gertrude Stein, *A Geographical History of North America*, 1934)

A re-appraisal of space

Changing technologies and living standards have caused Finns to pay increasing attention to space — air space above their country, working space, domestic space, personal space. Territorially speaking, Finland rejoices in having much more unoccupied space than occupied space. Population density, for what the measure is worth, is fifteen per square kilometre. It may be below the ideal of the American naturalist H.D. Thoreau (who preferred one inhabitant per square mile), but it is among the lowest ratios in Europe. Although population numbers are relatively stationary, population distribution tends to become increasingly uneven.

As one travels around Finland, it is surprising that such a visible impact over such an extensive area has been made by so few people. Nevertheless, the demand for living space and working space *per capita* and for space for the communications that link them grows ceaselessly, while the facility with which constructional activity is pursued advances simultaneously. As a result, the stock of older housing, older public buildings and industrial properties dwindles relatively, if not absolutely. The urban landscape of Finland, largely the product of the last generation, has a spick and span though often uniform appearance.

The bond with the land and its resources ties particular activities to particular places. An urban hierarchy has evolved in the process and, complementarily to it, a new attitude to the countryside. Ironically Finns are short of particular types of land for particular purposes, especially for leisure pursuits. An increasingly selective eye is cast over space. Above all, it is access to the waterside, in a country that has one of Europe's greatest lengths of coast and lakeshore per head of population, which has called for planning controls. Certainly, along Finland's littorals, coastal or lacustrine, there is more space where somebody is than where nobody is. It is another consequence of what has been called the collapse of space as a barrier.

A bond with the land

To have been introduced to Finland by those who have their roots in the land is inevitably to have experienced a measure of indoctrination. The *talonpojat* or *bönder*, mistranslated for decades as 'peasants' but more nearly approaching in status that of the British yeoman farmer, are no longer a dominant group in Finnish employment statistics. However, they continue to wield an influence out of all proportion to their numbers and their values are widely upheld. They have transmitted their philosophies and rustic truths. Their proverbs have been carried into urban contexts — *Oma tupa, oma lupa.**

Superficially, there is a uniformity about Finnish farmsteads. In fact, they vary considerably in size, composition and practice. Cultivated land is more extensive in the south: the forest component in the north. Mixed farming dominates, the proportion of animals in relation to arable area increasing northwards. The traditional division of labour between men and women has changed, although by comparison with much of Western Europe, women still play a greater part in animal husbandry. Historically, the horse was the animal with which the man was concerned. The machine that has replaced it is similarly a masculine preserve. Machines have also become status symbols. They have changed the farmer's concept of space and time.

Idealised — even idolised — it might be, but the family farm has nevertheless encountered burdensome times. As everywhere, farmers in Finland complain about their finances, but in few countries can there be such an elaborate and scientifically planned system of regionally adjusted subsidies. They worry about the weather, justifiably, although there are insurance schemes which their ancestors lacked. They suffer the problems of over-production. Concealed rather than revealed, there are abandoned fields, farmsteads and even settlements. The retreat has been especially pronounced in the north and north-east and in the outer archipelagos. True, child mortality has fallen, family size has declined and life expectancy has risen in these marginal areas, but the difference in living conditions between the most favoured and least favoured areas is large. It is often evident in the quality as well as the quantity of the amenities. The opportunities for supplementing farm incomes are also fewer on the margins of the economy.

Rural Finns are accustomed to close social bonding. 'Neighbours are the best guests' is a proverb not without reference to *talkoot*, the working bees which were once a characteristic of the countryside. They came into their own again during the resettlement years. The cooperative societies, the ramifications of which penetrate all areas of the rural economy, have

*Colloquially: In your own home you can do as you please.

different roots. They are marketing and sales organisations. Their familiar names are ecountered in every village, with well-known farmers on their boards. Their display stands often dominate the local shows sponsored by the regional agricultural societies. There are memories of interminable speech-making at the opening ceremonies of agricultural shows in Savo — as well as of infinitely polite committee meetings at Knipan in Ekenäs.

Each branch of farming has its cooperative association. It has been an experience to witness the rise — and decline — of fur farming. Visits to mink farms in Ostrobothnia and Åland over the space of several decades have offered the opportunity to see the transformation of a modest supplementary activity into a highly specialised pursuit with a product oriented to a world market. To the hybridised mink have been added hybridised foxes — and racoons. The square metres of Icelandic fish that were kept in refrigerated vaults in Åland have been succeeded by more elaborate dietary programmes. Boom conditions were marked by the erection of the immense fur auction centre at Vantaa and the purchase of the Hudson Bay marketing rights. Momentarily, Finland commanded the world fur market, but almost immediately the market showed a contraction in the face of Western Europe's response to the animal rights movement. To see a noteworthy enterprise challenged — to see high fences erected around the Vantaa centre — is to witness the sensitivity of yet another Finnish export to changes in consumer attitude and fashion.

All such enterprises reduce to a certain extent the mystique associated with the concept of farming. So do the pressures that spring from the internationalisation of marketing as well as the increasingly elaborate government support systems. Yet the outsider remains conscious that in Finland the family farm is still hallowed with something of a sacred quality. The steady stream of chronicles about families, homesteads, hamlets and villages that finds its way into bookshops reflects more than a concern for the countryside. *A Place of their Own*, to employ the title of Ray Abrahams's study of a declining farming community in north Karelia, is the kind of property that seems to nourish the soul if it does not always serve the needs of the body. And it is a nourishment which has somehow survived the redemptive process of land clearance to the lamented withdrawal from cultivation of land hard-won from the wilderness in living memory.

It is ironical that the steady increase in holdings deserted for economic reasons, with all the soul-searching that precedes such actions, is accompanied by the rapid multiplication of second residences — sometimes in the same areas. Seasonal migration has been a traditional feature of the rural economy. Two generations ago, cattle still moved to woodland shielings (revaluation of timber has largely eliminated the practice). In the archipelagos they might still also be seen standing patiently in rowing boats as they were transported to 'summer islands'. The summer migration of urban inhabitants is, paradoxically, a movement from amenity to more primitive conditions, from a protected environment to a more exposed setting. Somewhere a work of fiction is waiting to be written about the pains that offset the pleasures of owning a summer home.

The inhabitants of the fringes of settlement may also be migratory. To the north country belong adventurers — the woodsmen, the hunters, the gold panners, even an element of vagabondage. To the fringes of the urban south are appended the gypsies — *mustalaiset*, the dark people — of whom there are some 10,000. Their women command the scene — lace-bloused and necklaced above, swirling black skirt below ('How many metres of velvet?' asked the Fat Man on the Bicycle during his Finland visit. 'A dozen' was the reply, 'and I can only afford one skirt in a lifetime'). The gypsies haunt the market-places, stake out their quarters on the Baltic ferries, and congregate with their wares at strategic points in Stockholm. Society may disapprove, but they are also citizens of a common labour market. The world appears to be their oyster: a roof over the head matters less than the freedom to move.

A roof over the head

Memories of Finland are of places where people have lived, worked and worshipped and of the things that they have touched and used. Take a handful of examples.

There is Mannerheim's Helsinki residence — the colourful souvenirs of the remarkable ride through Asia contrasting with the austere bedroom and its uncomfortable bed. There is the apartment frequented by Lenin in Tampere. Did he really use that cutlery and that china on that table? There is Eino Leino's cabin at Jokela — the 'Einery-Leinery' to a generation of children who subsequently lived there as a summer retreat. There is the humble home of the Snellman family; a little short on artifacts. It contrasts with the old parsonage at Iisalmi, even more cosy than in Juhani Aho's day. There is Aleksis Kivi's shack in Nurmijärvi, with plenty of others of a similar character in the vicinity, some differing little in their primitive amenities until recent years. There is Sibelius's Ainola — no lake and no forest on the doorstep. There is Eliel Saarinen's superb Hvitträsk — fit home for Rapunzel or Péleas and Mélisande. The 'Empire-style' home of Runeberg in Borgå is typical of the modest patrician dwellings of the day which developed beyond the rambling alleyways that surrounded the cathedral. Rauma is a memory of comfortable clapboard houses behind the lace-curtained and flower-filled windows of which there is a flick of bobbins exploring some of the 400 pillow-lace designs mounted in the museum (is it really true that a lace handkerchief from Rauma in the breast pocket is a sign of a local dandy?).

In Finland's Bergslagen — Fagervik, Skogby, Antskog, Svartå — the mansions of ironmasters sit beside homes formerly occoupied by the hierarchy of smiths and the stables of their horses, with the dam that ponded back the water for the hammers providing a lake for appropriate swans. The imposing residences of later industrialists — James Finlayson's *palatsi* in Tampere, for example — have often been reduced in status, with offices and restaurants taking over. To the same category of dwellings belong the rural manor-houses, the *herrgårdar* or *kartanot*. Their *corps de logis* are a blend of the Chekovian and Strindbergian — communicating suites of rooms, a grand piano, rocking chairs, generous with unsprung furniture and family portraits, smelling of leather, cigars, coffee and faint perfume. Beyond the verandahs, invaded by honeysuckle, surrounded by phlox and tiger lilies, there are half-neglected gardens, bosky with fruit bushes, jungled with rhubarb, threaded with weedy paths, leading to fretworked gazebos. They suffer a whiff of decay from an age when time and space were measured in different labour costs. Contrastingly immaculate are the architect-designed residences of the captains of industry and commerce, perhaps most distinguished among them Alvar Aalto's Villa Mairea at Noormarkku.

Most Finns live in the well-built, well-designed, if somewhat monotonously similar red brick or colour-washed apartment buildings that have spread out in all directions from town centres. They are usually sensitively sited in relation to relief and existing vegetation. They are well maintained, well heated (increasingly by district heating) and well lit. They are mostly owner-occupied, with subsidised dwellings differing little in their appearance from those privately owned. In older city centres — Helsinki, Turku, Tampere — there is an old-established tradition of apartment houses — countyarded (the caretaker's family occupying the basement flat), stuccoed, but blissfully free from graffiti. It is often a long climb to the top floor, for many lack lifts. Zinc roofs may be silvery grey, dull red or inky-black. A fair number of the houses are the product of the *Jugend* period — perhaps more correctly the Finnish *Jugend* period, for is there any other country where the whimsical and frolicsome emblems of its style are so much in evidence? The decorative features are so prolific that the artistically-inclined visitor might well be recommended to seek entertainment by adopting a Johnny-head-in-the-air posture walking through neighbourhoods such as Eira, Kruununhaka and Katajanokka.

Indoors, stone treads of polished Gotland limestone, speared with fossils, lead to sturdy doors which may open upon high-ceilinged, parquet-floored rooms lit by the inevitable chandelier. There is an abundance of mahogany, a scatter of heirlooms and a touch of stained glass in windows

which often look out on to cavernous streets. In total contrast, except in
the age of the building, are the apartments — 120 of them — which have
been created out of the old Lapinniemi spinning mill in Tampere — a
conversion that anyone not fortunate enough to live there might have
cause to envy.

From their homes, there are libraries to which Finns may retreat. In a
country where literacy has long been prized, libraries and librarians are
held in high regard. The grandfather of libraries is that of the University of
Helsinki — a galleried, neo-classical gem into which all of the requirements of a modern library have been accommodated with difficulty, but
which has the unrivalled atmosphere which only generations of readers can
impart. In total contrast is the library of the city of Tampere — *Metso*, as it
is called after its 'grouse-shaped' ground plan. It is functionally effective,
visually imaginative and a tribute to the wisdom of the city fathers as well
as to its designers. Librarians have had a field day as university library has
been added to university library with the multiplication of institutions of
higher education. Specialisation has become inevitable. The library of
Rovaniemi, designed by Alvar Aalto as part of the city plan, has a section
devoted to the literature of Nordkalotten (Pohjoiskalotti). Its shelves
are heavy with every available relevant volume from Norway, Sweden,
Finland as well as Russia. In some libraries, there are little personal collections which have been lovingly accommodated. The new University
Library of Kuopio has a nook devoted to the collection of the Nobel
biochemist A.I. Virtanen. There are treasured private libraries — the
Armfelt collection at Åminne (evacuated to Sweden during the war years),
the Fiskars library in the manor-house of the old ironworks. Helsinki
University Library has a room devoted to the handsomely-bound Nicolaij
collection brought from the estate of Monrepos after the loss of Viipuri.

Churches account for some of Finland's oldest buildings. Archae-
ological remains attest that Sund church has existed on its present site for
a millennium. There are dozens of medieval churches. Brick-built Hattula
is more museum than church because of the richness of the *Biblia
pauperum* — its picturebook walls have been painstakingly released from
the desecrating limewash of the Reformation. In Taivassalo church, there
is a great mustering of saints. Around the coast, votive ships of the
seafaring fraternity multiply. Huittinen church has three. Kökar has a
model of an eighteenth-century warship presented as a token of gratitude
by two islanders who were rescued from Barbary pirates. Little Kumlinge
has anchors decorating the memorials to those lost at sea. In its churchyard, there are nautilus shells on the tombstones of former ships' captains.
Other churches owe their distinction to more recent artists. Haukipudas
rejoices in the tempera flights of imagination of Mikael Toppelius. At the
west end the Book of Genesis is the source of inspiration: at the east end,

the Book of Revelation. In between there is an interplay of vines and chinoiserie.

At Tornio a thin, shingled spire and bell-tower have pierced the northern sky for 300 years. Lemi is recalled for its white wooden church built on a great slab of rock in 1780. Kerimäki boasts the largest wooden church in the world. Its 3,400 seats are much appreciated by those who are crowded out of performances at the nearby Savonlinna festival. Pastel-coloured, unpretentious neo-Gothic clapboard churches, such as that at Suonenjoki, acquire a fairytale appearance in a winter setting. Picturesque bell towers and the occasional row of church stables (as at Närpes) add to the architectural interest. Some churches have antique wooden figures at their doors begging for alms. Nor must the sturdy parish granaries, many built 200 years ago or more against the threat of crop failure and famine, be forgotten. There are no less than 124 of them.

Orthodox churches are recalled — Hamina and Lappeenranta — their doors opening upon theatrical gilt and iconry. In total contrast is the decoratively restrained churches designed by Lars Sonck (Mariehamn springs to mind). The interior simplicity of Orivesi church is recalled. Alvar Aalto's ingenious design for the church at Vuoksenniska must command attention. On the other hand, a fair number of churches in the newer communities — perhaps for reasons of economy — bear an unfortunate resemblance to modified drill-halls or fire-stations.

Many visitors will applaud the church tax which, in addition to providing stipends, guarantees the maintenance of the fabric, the furnishings and the churchyards. Everywhere, the substantial granite memorials that mark family graves are accompanied by the rows of headstones, with their red rose bushes, that mark the last resting-places of men and women lost during the Russian wars. Finland has no Unknown Warrior's tomb with an eternal flame. Each and every warrior is remembered separately. It is a shock to see so many memorials to adolescents. Some particular cemetery will stand out in the memory of everyone. For no particular reason that of Sodankylä refuses to be forgotten.

And, lest we forget, there are the churches and cemeteries in lost Karelia that know no care, and the tens of thousands of burial mounds, now protected sites, in the Åland islands, which date from before the coming of Christianity and which have a sacred quality of their own.

A scatter of fortresses, made the prouder by their restoration, rival the oldest churches in age. There is magnificent Turku, the wartime damage to which called forth major reconstruction. Legendary Olavinlinna, once Sweden's most formidable fortress, is now opera's most eminent European outpost. Tavastehus, for long not especially well maintained, has been dragged into the late twentieth century by the restorers. The little island stronghold of Kajaani must be giddy with all the traffic that passes over the bridge above it. Raseborg, which remained persistently on European maps of Finland while more important places were omitted, is curiously off the tourist route. Kastelholm has retained much of its pastoral setting: Korsholm still seems to have been bypassed by time. Perhaps Viipuri's thirteenth-century fortress is on the way to being found again. The 1743 boundary has left its mark. The eyeless ruins of Lovisa's fortifications still make an impression. Eastwards Russia strengthened the strong-points of Lappeenranta, Taavetti and Hamina — the unusual wheel-shaped plan of which still controls the centre of the town. While the surveyors of *Finska recognoseringsverket* were identifying the inter-visible beacons along the border, Suvorov was strengthening the redoubts of Kärnäkoski, Järvitaipale, Utti and Liikkala. Today nature has largely taken them over.

Finland's most extensive stronghold — Suomenlinna/Sveaborg, created out of the rocky wastes of Vargskär — has also been its most fatal. British encyclopaedias described it as 'worthy of the Romans' — a fitting metaphor in that Ehrensvärd enjoyed his Rome. Its demise in 1808 has been equated with Sweden 'sinking permanently below the horizon'. On the seaward side of Suomenlinna there is an array of rusting cannons, mostly cast in Russia, with wild flowers pressing up to their muzzles . . . *Sanctus muros patriae*.

The shattered ruins of Bomarsund and its associated redoubts lost in surrounding forests tell of the fate of the last great fortress to be built on Finnish soil. They also speak of the last months before the Åland islands were demilitarised and internationally neutralised. Bomarsund has become not only a place of pilgrimage, but also one of theatrical entertainment. Quite different is the fate of the unexpected fortifications from the First World War. It is hard to think of the strategic planning that lay behind the construction of the outermost rim of the defences of St Petersburg in south-eastern Finland. Quite unexpected also are the débris-filled trenches, blasted out of the granite knolls beside which high-rise apartments sprout in Helsinki's Pohjois Haaga. They are as hidden as the circular *vallum* which may be discerned among the trees on Rapola hilltop, and which archaeologists attribute to the Iron Age.

More important for daily life are the places where Finns work. They have shown major changes in the span of forty years in response to increased national wealth and social legislation. There are the spick and span new industrial parks. There are the administrative buildings. The noble, if severe, façade of the Parliament House continues to survey a prospect of railway sidings; one day, they will be replaced. Engel's town hall in Hamina is memorable and Palmroth's prim frame building in Lappeenranta. Seinäjoki's civic centre remains architecturally stimulating; Tampere *talo* — all ceramic tile and glass — makes a staggering impact. The sturdy banks are remembered, seemingly run by ladies and unencumbered by the protective paraphernalia of less honest parts of the world. Investment in hospitals has obviously been enormous — from the prestigious structures that are tied to the medical faculties of the new universities to the charming children's hospital in Helsinki, with its bas-reliefs and memories of diminutive Professor Arvo Ylppö. Bastions of business, such as the Paasila/Fredriksberg complex and the sleek office buildings of provincial cities, are enlivened by colourful but discreet ribbons of neon lighting. The operators of retail stores have been slow to learn window-dressing skills. Contrastingly, international 'window-dressing' is developing into a fine art — certainly in the architecture of the Finnish pavilion for the Seville world's fair.

The tradition of functionally-designed factories — Sunila, Toppila, Varkaus, even Aalto's Vasa milk depot — has been extended to the production process on the shop-floor. Industrial design has become a way of thinking. The decades of success of Arabia are inseparable from the studios where individual artists have been given free play with their ideas. So, too, the workshops where fat cheeks blow glass. In total contrast are the dairies with their gleaming vats, pipes and tiles, and their laboratories filled with Finnish-designed equipment. Shipyards, with memories of the great covered yard at Sandviken a hive of warm activity in winter, contrast with the immense Neste refinery at Naantali, a fairyland of light when seen from the passing night-time ferry.

Places of entertainment leave their mark — symbols of national culture or provincial pride. The National Theatre in Helsinki must have been an extravagant investment in its day. It still stands the test of time and its solid granite structure may well be there when the contemporary city theatre has to be replaced. It has been fascinating to see the multiplication of civic halls and theatres in provincial towns — multi-purpose buildings to accommodate the diverse entertainments that move around the country — the conferences, too. For most Finns, the marble-clad Finlandia Hall is the home of music; but it is also the city's principal conference centre. To descend from the lofty to the lowly. Foreign visitors who patronise Finnish places of entertainment in winter never fail to be entertained by the expedition with which thousands of outer garments and overshoes are handled — and all free of charge.

Side by side with the rise of new buildings has been the refurbishment of old, sometimes in the face of opposition from progressive planners. Cities such as Turku illustrate the problem. Many of the old familiar buildings in the centre of town have been replaced by anonymous late twentieth-century structures. The old are lamented, but in most cases had outlived their useful life. At least the charming Swedish theatre has managed to resist destruction. There are also compensating gems of restoration. Craftsmen and craftswomen have lovingly restored the neo-classical observatory, right down to the gold stars in the firmament of the sky-blue cupola. But what can be done with the remains of the Dominican monastery, briefly opened up for archaeologists beneath the busy Kaskenkatu?

The creation of new working environments behind the façades of old respected buildings has gathered momentum. In Helsinki, it has been successfully applied to the city hall, the handicraft museum, the Ateneum and the old waterfront buildings of Katajanokka. It was a happy thought to bestow a facelift on the century-old market hall beside the south harbour. Tampere's programme of conversion and conservation also reflects the attempt to create something new out of the old and to maintain a harmony between the workplace and living space in the city of *Suomen Trikoo*, the lady with the golden thread.

The conservation of the old is inseparable from the folk museums, a Scandinavian feature which Finland has taken unto itself. Åbo's Klosterbacken/Luostarinmäki gives much pleasure. There are memories of its wooden workshops and dwellings, brought to life on Åbo Day by present-day craftsmen plying their trades in the cramped, dark and seemingly comfortless surroundings of times when living space had different dimensions. While Klosterbacken reflects the pre-industrial urban environment, Pielinen museum in north Karelia recalls the frontier of settlement. Here are juxtaposed the pioneering cabins, smoke-hole in roof, and the substantial homes of well-to-do farmers. Virsuvaara house displays the immense deal boards that were still available a century and a half ago, with the decorative axework then in fashion. To Pielinen have also been brought two loggers' camps which mark the advance from the primitive conditions of the 1930s to the somewhat improved state of the 1950s. Bear and wolf traps symbolise the presence of the natural frontier. What a contrast to the human chains displayed at the Museum of Ostrobothnia in Vasa on the more civilised coastland — chains kept for those who were unwise enough to use knives in public brawling.

The folk museums of eastern Finland have been journey's end for Matti Kaups and Terry Jordan from the United States of America in their search for the origins of the American log-cabin. Their quest led them from the shores of the Delaware by way of Swedish Värmland to Savo and Karelia, where they believe that they have found the answer.

A matter of communication

Within two generations Finland has witnessed the advance from a loosely structured transport network to the integrated system of a modern state. Man power, animal power and steam power have yielded precedence to other forms of traction. In the immediate pre-war years, there were still plenty of horse-drawn vehicles, even in the towns. Market squares had to make provision for the needs of horses and carts; army units still required stables; most farms used horses and they were critical for work in the forests (their winter shoes the counterparts of today's winter tyres).

Unsurfaced highways had yet to yield to tar-macadamed roads. In summer they were sprayed with a weak solution of chemicals to help lay the dust. Such surfaces were not very amenable to the heavy iron-framed bicycles of the day (pity the army conscripts). For those who had to use this form of transport there was a measure of relief when snow enabled it to be replaced by the *potkukelkka* (the history of which was sorted out in correspondence with Gösta Berg of Nordiska Museet in Stockholm in the 1960s). But for any form of transport, *kelirikko* — the time of freeze and thaw — disrupted transport on many roads for several weeks on end. Despite modern methods of construction, the springtime notices warning of frost upheaval still make their appearance along many highways.

It is only during the last forty years that ferries — some still manipulated by hand, others chugging with vehicles and livestock across lakeland narrows — have yielded to bridges. Sturdy little bridges built by the corps of engineers in the late eighteenth century along *Kuninkaantie*, the old royal road along the south coast, are still a happy sight. Shuddering wooden bridges in the post-war countryside are recalled. Most memorable is the trestle bridge — *Brändö bro*, creaking as trams to and from Helsinki, emptied of their passengers, passed warily over it. For an English visitor it had something of the appearance of Whistler's painting of Old Battersea Bridge. *Brandö bro* did its best to protect the sequestered villas of Brandö/Kulosaari from urban invasion. In vain, for a stream-lined motorway and an accompanying metropolitan railway now stride in a kilometre-long viaduct across the narrows. Meanwhile, in the coastal archipelagos, bridges leap from island to island, challenging the monopoly of the summer steamers and the need for winter highways across the ice.

Such developments are inseparable from the introduction of new concretes and cements — not least frost-resistant and fast-drying varieties (they recall visits to the limestone quarries of Parainen/Pargas and Lappeenranta/Villmanstrand). Cheap surfacing materials, derived from the by-products of the oil refinining industry, have been equally critical for road improvement. The contrast between the long, asphalted ribbon of the Arctic highway to Inari and the rough pre-war track to Petsamo is dramatic. The Tornio valley route to the west, leading to Finnmark and Troms, resembles a minor Alaskan highway. How different from the time when Maupertuis and his company of scientists, going north in 1735 to measure the passage of Venus, pushed and punted their boats through dozens of rapids and shallows up Tornio river to Aavasaksa.

Transport on the interior waterways has always been important — exhilarating perhaps for the tarboat operators who risked the hazards of the riverbeds on their way to the Ostrobothnian coast, exhausting for those faced with the daily chores in the rowboat. '*Akka soutamaan*' (the woman to the oars), says an old proverb — except on Sundays, when the men took to the churchboats. 'A hundred miles more or less by sea doesn't matter,' commented the Swedish administrator Jacob Faggot; but in the labyrinthine inland waters of Finland it mattered increasingly. Not surprisingly, the canal as a short-cut seized the imagination of late-eighteenth-century Finns. The corps of military engineers was summoned to prepare a scattering of plans (their fading outlines record canals and canalisation schemes, some undertaken and others discarded). The canalisation of parts of the Kokemäki river was begun and discontinued. C.F. Bremer heard from a British correspondent that it took 250 men three weeks to dig a mile of waterway in the English midlands; but the geology of Finland was somewhat different.

Frans Michael Franzén joined the enthusiasts. 'I am thinking of Canals in Uleåborg province,' he wrote from England in 1796. 'They could make a little Birmingham out of Kajaani: a little Bristol out of Uleåborg.' Saimaa Canal, *folie de grandeur* of Pontus de la Gardie with the remains of his 'ditch' marked by an historic plaque today, was a dream for more than two centuries before models of Neptune, Mercury and Väinämöinen presided over its opening in 1856.

In the post-war years, there has been another change in the appraisal of the inland waterways. Softwood bundles are still tugged across the lake systems on great rafts, seemingly at a snail's pace; but the sight of broad rivers choked with logs, often jammed at their sorting areas, has vanished. The log-sorters, both men and women, became the critical elements in the floatage operations. Exploiting their monopoly status, they priced themselves out of existence, with the result that most timber now moves from the forests to the processing plants overland. Timber companies arranged loans for smallholders to purchase lorries and to contract for roundwood transport. Accordingly, seasonal transport by water has been replaced by year-long movement by road.

Canal mania was succeeded by railway mania. From the outset the railway system was state-owned; it is heavily subsidised and there are elaborate freights rate differentials both to assist the movement of goods in the remoter parts of the country and to compensate areas which suffer from winter closure of ports. Speed is not a characteristic of Finnish railways, partly because of the nature of much of the road-bed. Peatland areas raise special problems. When the first fast train was introduced to the Kuopio route, it acquired the sobriquet *The Kalakukko flyer*, although in fact birds could fly past it. Much old rolling-stock and equipment remained in use until the post-war years — to the advantage of the railway museum at Hyvinkää. At a number of places — Pieksämäki and Kouvola are recalled — pensioned-off wood-burning locomotives have become part of the station scene. Their heavy diesel successors, drawing comfortable, curtained and air-conditioned coaches on the inter-city routes, are complemented by lighweight rolling stock for local services. Many original station buildings remain — in Empire style, neo-Gothic, Swiss chalet and Finnish *Jugend* with Helsinki the outstanding example (would that its architect had provided the platforms with more shelter from the elements). Around the country, station parks with raked gravel paths support occasional gazebos (that at Haukivuori appeals). Conversions are a tribute to architectural ingenuity. So are new station buildings, such as attractive little Humppilä. It is an agreeable experience to find efficient clerks, who seem to have no difficulty in reserving seats from anywhere to anywhere, and railway officials who seem proud of their uniforms. Most conductors are obviously appointed because of their avuncular mien. *Ravintola* coffee is excellent, of course. Although wheels may not fly as swiftly as the railway symbol suggests, Hermes serves Finland well.

By comparison, the atmosphere of the computer-designed ferries, built to carry millions (and their duty-free purchases) is that of a carnival. The great glass reception lounges at the quayside with their covered catwalks never cease to stir memories of former times. The post-war return to Turku was down an uncovered gangway to a down-at-heel immigration and customs shed, which still bore a cyrillic inscription from Russian days beside the Finnish and Swedish. The crossing in a quietly panting steamship, a tenth of the tonnage of present vessels, was a friendly experience. Even cabins privileged to have a porthole were doorless. Travellers were clearly more honest and certainly less intrusive than today. In the immediate post-war years they were often more hungry too. There might be as many as four sittings for dinner and, for those sufficiently affluent, a 6 o'clock dinner could be repeated at midnight. As the number of ferry-lines operating has increased, old familiar company names have gone through a series of changes.

Some of the original lakeland steamers, chicken-wired and smokestacked are still retained in service. They recall the leisurely movement at the turn of the twentieth century when local newspapers such as *Karjalatar* advertised timetables for *Kaleva* and *Wäinämöinen* from the lake ports of Saimaa to Viipuri, Koivisto and Pietari. Even Joensuu had an unexpected customs-house, a fleet of eighteen steamboats and eighty-six sailing vessels. Helsinki has its own relic from the past. *Johan Ludvig Runeberg*, held in affection by many, still plies a summer journey of four hours through the archipelago to Porvoo.

All this is a far cry from the services offered by Finnair, the national airline, which has already passed its diamond jubilee. Finnair, which provides an intensive internal network to more than twenty destinations, has more than fulfiled the fantasisings of a contributor to *Helsingfors Tidningar* in 1860: Simon Lewis, an agent of Rothschild's banking house in London, was supposed to travel to Finland to gain an impression of the country before a loan was made, and he journeyed round in an 'air clipper' called *Ilmatar*. In the 1990s he could start with any one of three planes a day from London (accompanied by the unseen freight that brings profit to the route). The domestic routes must benefit from a high proportion of official travellers — even university staff moving between campuses. Given such facilities, it is not unusual to work in the north of Finland and to live in the south — especially when wives may occupy position of similar status and remuneration to their husbands'. Air transport has changed working practices as well as concepts of time and space. Peripherality in Europe has become relative for Finland. It is evident in the daily air connection between Rovaniemi and Murmansk, which begins to make the Murmansk *oblast* feel a part of the Finnish hinterland. Geographically, the relationship is comparable to that between Finnmark and the rest of Norway.

A further significant change in Finnish communications must be recorded. In the 1940s, many parts of the countryside still had telephone exchanges located in private homes, the operators of which were alerted by callers vigorously turning a handle on their domestic apparatus. Today Finland has an international reputation for its contributions to telecommunications, not least for its large-scale mobile telephone output and experimental telephone screens.

An urban hierarchy

Finnish urbanists have conceived a hierarchy of towns based on population numbers, the networks of communications that link them together and the zones of influence that they command. The system derives principally from the central place-theory of the German geographer Walter Christaller, who himself visited Finland before the Second World War and whose ideas have not been without influence in the successive post-war changes in local government boundaries.

Helsinki remains Finland's leading city. Turku, which lost its administrative function after 1812 but still retains the archbishopric, is only a fifth of its size. Bustling Tampere, a parvenu by comparison, rivals Turku for second place in the population race. The provincial capitals, old and new, have all gained in importance through the recasting of local government authority. The fortunes of lower-ranking settlements have had their ups and downs. Ostrobothnia's small and medium-sized manufacturing centres are almost unknown by name internationally, but they are unconcerned by the world's ignorance because they tend to thrive in spite of it. Contrastingly, the one-industry softwood settlements, often well-known by the outside world through the names of their products, find that of little comfort when the market slumps. The same applies to the handful of mining towns, which are the more apprehensive of their future in the light of the finite character of their resources.

Modest settlements are remembered which were more ambitious in the past. They included pleasingly superannuated trading places along the Bothnian coast — Kristinestad/Kristiinankaupunki, Kaskö/Kaskinen, Kalajoki and Iijoki. For the casual summer visitor they seem to be all the better for time having passed them by.

Some towns owe their existence to more recent economic theories. They are illustrated by Kemijärvi, where a large softwood processing plant was created to stimulate employment in an underdeveloped area. Similar motives lay behind the establishment of the state-owned iron and steel plant at Rauttaruukki and the ferro-steel plant near Tornio. Growth centre theory also part explains the establishment of new universities at Oulu in north Finland and Joensuu in the east.

Formal town planning began in Finland in the seventeenth century. In Raahe evidence can still be seen of the geometrical pattern of streets focusing on a central square, with its church and town hall, and each residential lot identified (conveniently for taxation purposes) and each property defined about its central yard or garden. For Kokkola/Karleby, a succession of documents, used in the *Scandinavian Atlas of Historic Towns*, illustrates the persistent influence of the original plan.

Already in the eighteenth century, roads were being widened in towns to reduce the risk of fire. What Nathaniel Hawthorne in New England considered 'purification by fire' may have had hygienic benefits, but it caused great personal anguish and destroyed much of aesthetic value. Turku was both straitened and straightened after the fire of 1827. Old Vasa was replaced by Nikolaistad after the fire of 1852 — a bronze plaque recalls its original plan. In turn, Nikolaistad became new Vasa, with its principal planning concern the construction of a succession of harbours to keep pace with the emerging shoreline and the increasing size of shipping.

The wartime firing of Rovaniemi was deliberate, but at least the *tabula rasa* provided Alvar Aalto with the opportunity to design the capital of Lapland anew. . . . And yet Rovaniemi might have been an experimental winter city — perhaps rechristened Arctopolis (a name that atlas-makers once accorded to Pori). The medieval *bastide* might have been taken as a partial model — its fortifications against climate rather than against men. Modern Rovaniemi is not an ideal city for high latitudes. The distances between residential areas, shops, entertainment and transport centres represent winter tracts of sub-Arctic desert between super-heated oases. It might have been a more compact, cosier place with a warren of narrow streets, with walkways (as in Minneapolis) between tower blocks and service centres, with railway, bus and car services underneath. It is a place where the imagination can be allowed to run riot. Since Rovaniemi has become the centre of Father Christmasland, it has the potential for developing a veritable theme-park. . . . A palace for the Snow Queen? Golden reindeer for Sampo Lappelil and white reindeer for Yrjö Kokko? Adventurings from Kalevala's Pohjola, the North Country?

But to return to reality. The climax of formal planning came with the grand project drawn up for Helsinki by Johan Albrecht Ehrenström. Much pleasure has been derived from it aesthetically — and practically. Captain Jones, passing through Helsinki in 1827, was delighted when Carl Ludvig Engel showed him the plans for further 'improving and embellishing the town'. It pleased Sven-Erik Åström to write about them in a fuller historical context for the city's four hundredth anniversary, while a later reproduction of the plans and designs in a handsome format has given wider access to the treasured originals.

The kind of order imposed on the peninsular site by Ehrenström and Engel has been interpreted by some as an expression of the political controls prevailing at the time. Certainly, the nineteenth-century architecture and plan of Helsinki reflect features of St Petersburg — or, perhaps, the European influence as expressed in St Petersburg. Be that as it may, the introduction of the neo-classical style by Engel made significant contributions by example to architecture elsewhere in the Finnish urban scene.

In the original plan of Helsinki the 'stone' quarter, with its public buildings, military section and administrators' residences, was complemented by the 'wooden' quarter, with its artisan dwellings and workshops. While the latter has been replaced, the former is carefully — and extravagantly — maintained. The approach from the sea can still be dramatic. Frans Michael Franzén was enraptured at the sight when he paid a visit in 1842. The dome of the great white church dedicated to St Nicholas, rising up out of the sea mist, appeared 'as at the rubbing of an Aladdin's lamp'. The illusion can still be repeated. Other visionaries have conceived plans for the expanding capital. To visit Munkkiniemi is to be reminded momentarily of Eliel Saarinen's Greater Helsinki plan of 1918. To sit on the balcony of a frame-house in Käpylä amid apple tree tops and swaying birches is to reflect on the good fortune that has protected its 1920s character from developers. Less happy has been the lot of Lars Sonck's early villa oasis of Kulosaari — its early vision recorded for posterity by Laura Kolbe. Tapiola, the garden suburb on a grand scale, is unique. To the outsider, it appears to be a highly successful enterprise, only lacking the amenity of a metro extension. And all the time, it is to be hoped that one day the essentials of Aalto's plan for central Helsinki will be fulfilled.

Civic pride runs strongly through Finland: inter-city rivalry is often intense. Amenities benefit correspondingly, from street furniture to public parks. Helsinki led the way with the first public parks — Kaivopuisto/ Brunnsparken and Töölö/Tölö. The model, strangely enough, lay in Birkenhead — another Finnish link with Merseyside. The pioneer was Henrik Borgström, who spent a year learning the essentials of trade in Liverpool. His bust stands in Eläintarha park, near clusters of rhodedendrons which somehow manage to survive. Park-keepers struggle bravely with their responsibilities, for the Finnish winter is hard on plant life. Not for Finland the age-old lawns of Western Europe. Regular seeding is necessary and the close shave of a modern motor-mower can be fatal.

Leisureland

In the space of two generations Finland has become very much a leisure-land. Thanks to the regulation of working hours and the guarantee of extended holidays, all classes of society may now be termed leisured as the word was understood by Thorstein Veblen. Finns have time to play, or to stand and stare should they prefer, because they need less time to make a living than formerly. Moreover, most have a surplus of energy which must in some way be released. In the span of two generations sport has become professionalised and ritualised.

Sometimes it seems as though the work ethic has been stood on its head. City residents buy forest lots not only as investments but for the pleasure of labouring in them for exercise. The Arctic Canoe Race on Tornio river calls for stamina greater than that of the boat men whose skills brought tar barrels over the rapids of the Oulu river to the coast. Logging competitions provided even more arduous challenges than the logging operations of former times. Orienteering has become a fiercely competitive sport. Wilderness trails encourage trekking that would call for protective legislation were it required of a workforce. The winter extraction of ice blocks, with man-sized saws, for storage in ice-houses was hard labour: contemporary competitive ice sculpting is regarded as play, laborious though it may be. Gold panning in mosquito-ridden Lapland, once the pursuit of a hardy handful of adventurers, is presented as a tourist pursuit. The spring over-haul of pleasure-boats and their inevitable engines is treated as a labour of love, although the autumn hauling ashore and wrapping up for the winter are willingly left to others if the purse permits. The discipline of the yacht crew is accepted happily even though it may well be fiercer than that experienced by the naval conscript. Dragnet fishing beneath the Baltic ice is no longer commercial viable, but for all the modern conveniences surrounding it, *pilkki kalastus* or icehole fishing is not exactly a comfortable activity. Competitive enthusiasm probably generates enough heat to attract the 5,000 participants in the annual *pilkki kalastus* marathon. Rod and line, net and trap are part of the clutter in most summer homes: so also, in the Åland islands, are the crayfish nets. Fish farmers provide increasing sport for impatient anglers, with salmon and trout for all to catch, to be weighed, gutted and paid for on the spot.

Hunting no less than fishing is a birthright for this nation of Nimrods. Both are for early risers, for whom, in the words of J.V. Snellman, 'the dawn has gold in its mouth'. Hunting means shooting, and shooting is a seasonal pursuit. It was a necessity in the past, especially in the so-called 'years of the wolves' which persisted well into the nineteenth century. The marksman at his best, according to O.F. Wetterhoff, was a Savolaxer who could 'shoot a squirrel in the eye while skiing'. The elk remains the principal quarry and, to keep numbers down, must be culled annually by the thousand. Although it is generally asserted that there is nothing worth shooting on four legs between a hare and an elk, there are plenty of wild deer — and even foxes. The first brochures of the Finnish Tourist Association in 1895 intimated that bear hunting 'could be arranged' — and the presence of bearskins in many country homes suggests the widespread distribution of a dangerous animal. Today the bear is a protected species, but from time to time culling is needed. In any case, bear steaks appear on the menus of exclusive city restaurants, though they may reflect a hard currency export from the east.

Game birds are at their fattest as autumn approaches, with the blackcock probably the best. Migrant birds call for migrant shooting parties. Hailuoto may beckon when the geese migrate, and the south-west marshes when the wild duck are on the wing.

In the last half-century, *homo ludens fennicus* has become increasingly professional. Leisure pursuits remain a nice blend of the individual and the collective, but they are steadily diversified and call for increasing investment of capital. Participation is the order of the day, but spectators multiply in a nation which has come to worship athleticism and for which the word Olympic has become emotionally charged. Team games keep everybody happy, with increasingly elaborate sports halls taking over when outdoor matches become impossible. *Pesäpallo* has emerged as a national sport, claiming more spectators than football, though the presentation of British League tables on television and their recitation on the radio proclaim an international interest in a sport which probably had its Finnish origins among British entrepreneurs in Helsinki several generations ago. Permanent grass may be unhappy in Finland, but that does not prevent golfers from multiplying their courses.

It is natural that it should be in winter sports that the nation excels. To cross-country skiing around the home area have been added the temptations of the burgeoning Lapland resorts, where a measure of elevation is offered for downhill runs. The older ski resorts in Salla and Kuusamo have witnessed the appearance of the fun-and-games centre at Rukatunturi, which was wilderness two generations ago. *Erämaa herättää*, the wilderness stimulates — so it used to be said. A contrasting kind of stimulus is provided by the complex of hotels, hostels and second homes at Saariselkä — seemingly a conspicuous investment in leisure alien to the area. It is conceived as a stimulus to activity in a territory of traditional unemployment. In fact, Lapland is large enough to accommodate it. Happily, the northland at large is unlikely to become a destination for mass tourism.

'Man only plays when he is in the fullest sense of the word a human being and he is only fully a human being when he plays.' In the light of Schiller's aphorism, late twentieth century Finns must be aware that never in the life of the nation have they had the opportunity to fulfil themselves so completely as human beings.

7

THE STATE OF THE ARTS

'Perfection just precedes change.' (A.N. Whitehead)

The art of living

In Finland the art of living resembles that of its Scandinavian neighbours. So too does its social vision. It is a welfare state. Much of its social legislation is in common with that agreed by members of the Nordic Council. Finnish society is egalitarian, yet it is not without consciousness of its hierarchies and antecedents. *Kuka kukin on* is an indispensable Finnish *Who's Who*.

At the same time, the little red book of the *Finlandsadels kalender* is still very much in print. Family coats of arms are reproduced beside the entries, they crowd the walls of the old House of the Nobility, they persist in the faded armorial bearings that are to be found in medieval churches. Genealogists thrive — and not only for domestic reasons. There are memories of the family tree of the Ramsays. During a visit to Henrik Ramsay an anecdote about Sir William Ramsay was recalled. William Ramsay the chemist, became interested in the Finnish branch of his family, and in 1909 made a summer pilgrimage with his wife to re-establish his ancestral links, and to be welcomed by his kinsmen on the quayside. The memoir of his visit is among the Ramsay papers at University College London.

The professions, accessible to all with talent, still tend to breed dynasties. There are ecclesiastical dynasties which circulate around the parsonages of substantial parishes. They may not be family preserves as much as in the past, but following father into the 'trade' (mother too these days) is common. There are university, legal and medical dynasties. There are minor dynasties of craftsmen and artists as well as of merchants, such as the furriers and jewellers whose ancestral roots were in St Petersburg. There are dynasties of market traders — fishwives and fruiterers, market gardeners and coffee vendors — genial as any in the world. Tuula Tiitinen's sunny portrait of *Torimummo* commanding the market place is their epitome.

All of which turns thoughts to the Finnish face, a feature which awaits appraisal in the way that Kenneth Clark treated its English counterpart. The Finnish face is described verbally in many encyclopaedias, but without much prospect of recognition. It stares boldly from advertisements. It is caricatured by cartoonists. Erkki Tanttu's simple line drawings epitomise the earthy country folk. Albin Kaasinen has captured the same people in his

wood carvings. Artists have immortalised the faces of ordinary people —
the portraits of Juho Rissanen and Magnus Enckell spring to mind. Hugo
Simberg's *Akseli* positively haunts. Formidable family photographs claim
wallspace beside the likenesses (and unlikenesses) by portrait painters to
whom Finns would seem to offer endless commissions. Ethnic homo-
geneity suggests that there ought to be an 'Identikit' Finn, but there is
not. In any case, a portrait is a static thing and a face is dynamic. Even the
finest artist cannot capture the dancing eyes of a Karelian.

Nor do Karelian eyes and temperament tally with the taciturnity that
some outsiders have ascribed to the Finn. A book may have been written
on the silent Finn, but its author must have sought the characteristic
among the minority of solitary and seemingly unattached men who, having convinced the bouncers at restaurant entrances of their credentials, sit
alone with their preferred beverage gazing into space. In fact, Finns can be
downright loquacious, children as well as adults.

Finland is very much a childrens' country. Children are less fussed over
and much more taken for granted than in many lands. In the countryside,
especially, women accept the additional burden of children as something
natural. Aleksis Kivi's metaphor — born between the rocks and the
strawberries — may be poetic licence, but there is an element of truth
in it. In towns, most men seem to accept a greater share of the responsibility for young children. There is no male hesistancy about pushing
perambulators and push-chairs. In any case, there is the corpus of park
aunts to hand, without whose labours there would be fewer working
wives.

The liberation of Finland's young has been an easier process than in
many West European countries. The drift to the towns, which in any case
lack the urban excesses of Western Europe, has not commonly severed the
link with the countryside. Much more important, the possibility of
sharing in the good things — even what in some cases might seem to be
the extravagant things — of life is greater. For example, winter sports and
water sports are available to all. The possibilities for getting rid of surplus
energy in a positive manner and in situations which are the reverse of
socially divisive cannot fail to dissipate adolescent stresses.

There are also rituals, some still shared with the entire family, which
retain an appeal for the young. The midsummer bonfire is a universal
celebration. The preparation of midsummer poles in Åland, seemingly
topheavy with elaborate decorations, is a cooperative pursuit. *Vappu*, May
Day, following Walpurgis night, might seem to have been created for the
young, especially the young who have matriculated. It appeals no less to
the young in heart, grey-headed though they may be. A holiday mood
prevails. Yellowing student caps, some half a century old, are given an
airing. Balloons are everywhere. Past May Days in Helsinki are also

recalled for the incongruous note struck by the red flags, banners and brass bands of the Communist processions passing through the city centre.

Christenings and confirmations bring families together. A surprising 90 per cent of children are christened and an equal number confirmed. Confirmation camps retain an unusual appeal. The laying on of hands is as big a social event as ever, with the confirmation presents advertised in the press sometimes attaining extravagant proportions. White for the girls and dark blue for the boys is *de rigueur*. White and black continue through life's rituals. White wedding dresses are complemented by white tie and tails: widows may still wear black, even veils. Fringed and fluted crisp white coffins sit in the dark premises of undertakers. Snowstorms and frozen soil may delay burials in winter. Eighty per cent of weddings are conducted in church; for funerals the proportion is 95 per cent.

And the spruce shares in many of these occasions. It may form an archway over the door at wedding receptions. When there are celebrations, it may be spread as a welcoming mat on the threshold. It comes into its own at Yuletide — festooned in the streets. Traditionally it has decorated the four corners of the funeral carriage.

In general, there is not much churchgoing, although seasonal festivals attract large numbers of what otherwise appears to be a secularised society. Church services are cast in an old familar mould. Modern clerics are more restrained than in the days when Amelia Herbert wrote, 'The Finnish preacher can be heard a *verst* off.' Church music is primarily in the minor mode. Hymns, gathered together in a new hymnal and printed like Anglican psalms, are sung seated and there is no kneeling except at the altar rail. Not much joy seems to be registered; but, churchgoing and outward joyfulness are not necessarily linked. However, social discipline is presumed to derive in part from the Lutheran tradition, perhaps also a measure of scepticism.

Scepticism seems to be cast aside and discipline happily embraced in one area of national life. The willingness to undertake the obligation of military service exceeds that in any other country where there is conscription. Fully 90 per cent of young males accept the nine-month commitment.

While members of the armed services bear their standards and salute the flag, for others the flag is an indispensible feature of daily life. The number of flagpoles in Finland must exceed even those in other Nordic countries. On national days and official occasions, on high days and holidays, responsible authorities, armies of caretakers and private citizens unfurl them with zeal. Flags are hoisted widely to welcome; they are found amid the candles in restaurants and hotels. The province of Åland flies its own flag, incorporating the colours of the old Swedish flag and the blue and white of

Finland. Durable though fabrics may be, wind, rain and chemical weathering must take their toll. The wear and tear is greater still for the flags and pennants that flutter on the tens of thousands of boats. Flag production must be a profitable business in Finland.

Flags may speak a language or simply have an aesthetic appeal. They express the happy juxtaposition of the formal and informal that characterises Finland. There are vivid memories of the formality of doctoral examinations, held in public with radio and television at the ready. For the candidates, they must constitute a form of pillory. The ceremonies associated with doctoral 'promotions' carry formality to a climax, with a *major domo* (Ole Reuter will always be remembered), with top hats and swords, orders and decorations, banners and sashes, processions and pronouncements, sermons and music. It is pleasant to find Latin retaining a place in them as an honoured language (honoured, too, in that there is a Latin translation of *Kalevala* and even a Latin news bulletin on the radio). Nor is the dancing (in Helsinki at any rate) that succeeds the academic 'promotion' free from formality. To the accompaniment of a military band, there is a carefully rehearsed programme which runs through the polonaise, quadrille, *pas de quatre*, chaconne and other set dances to the final valse. In the Helsinki ceremony, dawn breaks and, weather permitting, the dance takes to the Esplanade, with a final polonaise behind the residual instrumentalists.

Surprisingly, there is also formality in the terms of personal address. Titles are acquired rather than inherited, but they still identify the kind of social distinction unexpected in an egalitarian society. Plain *herra*, *rouva* or *neiti* are commonly replaced by an occupational title. The master's degree from the university carries with it the respected *maisteri/magister*. In keeping with the state university system, professors receive their letters of appointment from the President. The honorary title of professor, awarded for distinguished services, is an appealing institution. The coveted title of *neuvos/råd* (untranslatable because it does not exist in the English-speaking world) is the very pinnacle of distinction. The polite form of address in the third person, employing if need be simply the title, sounds curiously archaic, but it has its uses and conveniences. The use of Christian names, once upon a time delayed until a sauna was shared or a number of drinks consumed, has become increasingly common.

Much is made of anniversaries — indeed, they can be almost an obsession. The rows of Finnish faces that appear in daily papers and weekly journals advertising yet another quinquennial or decennial birthday anticipate open house, coffee for all and flowers for male and female alike. Name days, most of which have long been in the church almanack, are also remembered. The time has long since passed when the amateur poet's offering of a name day verse was adequate. Today, they are a profitable business, and there is no excuse for overlooking them because the radio gives them a leading place before the morning news bulletin.

There is no more agreeable formality than that expressed by flowers. Flowers are given with a frequency and generosity matched by few other countries, if any. The height of latitude or the severity of the season make no difference. The range of flowers available has become increasingly varied, and the sources of supply increasingly exotic. Is there any country outside the tropics, where orchids are so abundant as in the flower shops of Finland? It can only be assumed that they fill any spare capacity on long-haul air routes. And from where do all the roses come that are essential at times of matriculation and graduation? Clearly florists in Finland are a unique breed: they are either born to their trade or carefully educated in the art of handling customers — holding up individual blooms with an admiring eye, assiduously adding to them, proferring a little foliage to fill the gaps, wrapping scanty bouquets in substantial layers of paper. The ritual is identical in the brightly lit flower booths, electrically heated when winter takes over, which remain open long after shops are closed.

There is a memory of formal flower beds — stiff red cannas resisting sea breezes — at Kultaranta. Following a bus ride to Naantali, there was a walk along the drive post the empty sentry box. A lone soldier, suddenly realising that he was responsible for security, trundled informally after us on a bicycle, accepted the fact that we had been invited to tea, remained unconcerned about the contents of our briefcases, and retreated. More formally, an equerry waited by the villa: informality itself, President Paasikivi joined us. There was a long teatime chat in a room piled high with books. *The Times* (read daily) lay open on a nearby table. The central question (to vindicate an answer given at the Royal Geographical Society the previous year): 'How was the 1944 Karelian boundary defined?' The reply: 'Stalin simply drew a line on a map and the boundary was expected to follow it on the ground.'

The ultimate Finnish informality is born of the sauna, although it is hedged around with rituals of varying character. The sauna is at once a barbaric and a civilising institution. It is difficult to use titles in the nude; it is impossible to be impolite. An English friend experiencing her first sauna was not a little surprised when a naked Finnish girl entered and bobbed her a curtsey. Beyond the sauna, the lake awaits — the shower, the swimming pool, the snow, the ice-hole. At the Sauna Society, the muscular unseeing sauna ladies wait by their marble slabs. With due formality and unembarrassed, no matter how shapeless their clients, they undertake their shrivings.

The paramountcy of education

To visit Finland is to become aware of the attention paid to education. There is no great trumpeting of the fact that a fifth of the state expenditure is devoted to it. The results are evident both to see and to hear. With the German tradition as a model and that of Sweden as a challenge, there can never be any fear that Finland would fall behind in the world's educational stakes. Finland is neither too big to suffer from the centralisation of the educational system nor too bureaucratically restrictive to inhibit diversification. Academic standards are high. In so far as there is élitism in Finland, it is closely associated with the universities. Historically, they have been regarded as a route to advancement, especially for the sons of farming families, although daughters are probably equal in number to their brother students today. If, as sometimes happens, members of the international community adopt a somewhat patronising attitude to the Finnish academic scene, they rapidly discover the error of their ways, for the international intellectual aristocracy has its quota of Finns. Reciprocally, Finns have their own prestigious Academy of Science and Letters.

A well-established tradition in technical and vocational education has paid handsome dividends as Finland has moved forward into the technological age. The Technical University at Otaniemi in the garden city of Tapiola, the planning of which provided the architectural fraternity with a field day, now competes with the technical departments of the new universities. Higher vocational training has an established place in adult training, with a carefully graded scale of grants to help mature students. A remarkable 20 per cent of university entrants arrive by the vocational route. Not surprisingly, a national concern with agriculture spurred the establishment of an institute of advanced studies at Mustiala a century and a half ago. The needs of ordinary country folk have been equally recognised. To the folk high schools have been added special schools catering for smallholders, dairy farmers, foresters and even fur farmers. The status of handicraft schools, with the range of their finely crafted products much extended through the decades, has never been higher.

In the schoolroom, where there is not a uniform in sight, there is nevertheless a distinct sense of formality. The status of the teaching profession is high; and to this, discipline in the educational field is clearly related. Once, two dozen stereotype landscapes of Finland by the artist Vihtori Ylinen used to hang on the walls of all primary schools — visual images of the home country. They have become collectors' items. The engravings and enlarged photographs of the founding fathers of Finland may no longer cast a disciplinary eye down from the walls of assembly halls, but an official portrait of the President claims a prominent place. By comparison with the standards in many parts of Europe, the fabric of schools is well maintained (winter demands it). Equipment would make many visiting teachers envious. Throughout the nine years of compulsory schooling which starts at the age of seven, there are competitive examinations. They seem to cause no undue psychological stress. Considerable respect is attached to the matriculation examination. Half of the matriculating students enter university institutions.

The increase of institutions of higher education to twenty has barely kept pace with student demand. Numbers have increased fourfold to 100,000 in forty years. The universities of Oulu, Jyväskylä and Tampere have been joined by those of Joensuu and Vaasa, while additional faculties have given new institutions to Kuopio, Lappeenranta and Rovaniemi. The Institutes of Translation Studies, as at Kouvola, Turku and Savonlinna, are much valued additions. Language, once a sufficiently vexed issue to lead to the establishment of separate Finnish-language and Swedish-language institutions and to call for manifold compromises in the appointment of university staff, has lost most of its ability to generate rancour. Now it is the intrusive English language which raises problems — English ousting Swedish, English pushing aside German. The bank loans that tide over undergraduate and postgraduate years do not seem to inhibit the demand for learning, but they must take the edge off domestic relations, often constituting a mortgage worse than one arising from bricks and mortar.

At the postgraduate level, it has been gratifying to see a reduction in the size of the formerly very weighty doctoral dissertations without seeing a decline in their quality. Certainly the experience of assessing post-doctoral candidates for international fellowships suggests that the standard of Finnish applicants is second to none.

The procedures for filling university posts naturally differ from country to country, but the results can arouse the same passions. Experience in Finland (and Sweden) suggests that there might be something to be said for retaining the confidentiality of the reports on candidates submitted by external experts. It is not easy to be both frank in comments and resilient enough to withstand the lingering animosity that often results. The passage of a generation has reduced the gulf that used to exist between professors and students, but it is still not easily bridged. The hierarchy of university teachers seems to be jealously guarded, with a prestige being attached to chairs that no longer exists in many countries.

There is one corner of the University of Helsinki where the professoriate at one time must have sensed a yawning gulf between its body and ultimate authority. It is the alcove which contains the gilt-framed full-length portraits of the five Russian emperors who were the successive chancellors of the Imperial Alexander University. They are a colourful company who put in the shade their successors' portraits in the University consistorium. At the same time, there comes the sobering response that it was during the chancellorship of the last Tsar that many of Finland's university men were exiled to Siberia. Suddenly, thoughts turn to the obelisk at the Luumäki railway station which marks the point of departure of one of them — Ukko-Pekka Svinhufvud, who was later to become President of Finland.

Between 1968 and 1972, a research seminar on Finland was held at the School of Slavonic and East European Studies in London. In 1969, Anthony Upton delivered a memorable paper. He identified a number of characteristics of the Finnish university system and sought an explanation for them. It was for long a 'small closed system . . . with a premium on conformity' and with an academic establishment which was 'in law and spirit an important part of the official structure of the Finnish state'. Indeed, in some respects the academic community was the 'guardian of the national culture'. The curiously close association between intellectual circles and the state implied that the university itself became a symbol of power. It was regarded as near subversion for the young to stray from the paths of orthodoxy. The reaction during the years of student rebellion was correspondingly stronger. The subsequent liberalisation of the universities owes something to the internationalisation of Finland, of which student revolt was in some respects an early expression.

The importance attached to education helps to explain why Finland is such a literate country. Historically, the church played a pedagogical role; subsequently, literacy has been a powerful force in the establishment of the nation state. Literacy is writ large in the Finnish home. It almost seems as though there is a competition to see who subscribes to the largest number of newspapers, magazines and journals or who can claim the most metres of bookshelves. Given the changing economic situation, it was clearly impossible for the large number of newspapers that existed a generation ago to be maintained. If it was sad to see the demise of *Uusi Suomi*, it has been gratifying to witness the rise of *Helsingin Sanomat* (and to hear the unbelievably early clatter that announces its delivery through the letterbox of the average Helsinki apartment).

Living among displaced Karelians in the difficult post-war years, it was remarkable to see as many as a dozen different publications delivered weekly to the postbox. The physical effort of land clearance appeared to stimulate the need for mental activity when the lamp was lit. The eagerness with which the travelling library was awaited remains despite the lure of television. The hunger for books is reflected in the number of borrowings *per capita* from public libraries. In Europe, only Denmark rivals Finland.

The spare and the elegant

In the Finnish educational system, there is much that is enviably extravagant for the outsider. In the applied arts, there is much that is elegant because it is spare, a characteristic which probably reflects past economy inherited by present practice. Concern with design is inseparable from the old craft schools. It is a far cry from the first spinning and weaving school established on the Benvik estate near Kristinestad in the early nineteenth century or from the diligently propagated arts and crafts undertaken by the Finnish Economic Society to the present situation. In Finland, design and industrial process have operated in harmony more commonly than in most other developed countries. This is probably because the artist craftsman or craftswoman frequently occupied an established place in the community before large-scale industrial development took over. From the beginning such people, aware of the restraints imposed on Finland by its limited range of raw materials, have made the maximum use of the minimal opportunities available to them. Thus contemporary technology, by extending the range, has favoured Finland disproportionately by comparison with some parts of the world. Anything which diversifies the resource base opens up new prospects.

'Perfection just precedes change'. One reason for employing the Whitehead epigraph is that it expresses a personal feeling about much in the field of the applied arts in Finland. Time cannot stand still and perfection is a matter of individual taste. The disappearance of particular products which seems to have reached perfection is not unique to Finland. Market forces demand different designs, so that change for its own sake may imply the inferior replacing the superior. It is a difficult problem. A personal reaction to the shape, substance and decoration of several ceramic products illustrates the point. Friedl Kjellberg's so-called 'rice' design may have been somewhat precious (and it was for foreigners at least rather expensive), but it was unique, and the presence of even a single example immediately excites the interest of those who have never previously seen it. The unusual tableware, with F. Tengström's engravings on a white surface to commemorate the four hundreth anniversary of the foundation of Helsinki, is much admired but seems to have disappeared from ceramic departments. The coffee cups alone, just the right size, never cease to arouse comment. Soon after the late 1940s there disappeared from stores another Arabia product — the perfect breakfast cup and saucer. It was pale blue in colour, with a suggestion of transparency in the glaze through to a terracotta base ('Where *do* they come from?' asks an admirer 'From the past', must be the reply). Much admired Arabia *Ruska* is still with us, somewhat on the heavy side but calculated to attract attention beyond Finland. Indigo and white *Valencia* has Finland written all over it: *Paratiisi* (Paradise), too. Both demonstrate that perfection is still achievable.

As with Sweden, glass design in Finland is not always what it was. Genius has a habit of exhausting itself. Alvar Aalto's amoeba-shaped Savoy vase is one of the ultimate pieces of Finnish design — a collector's piece.

The more it is seen, the greater appears the elegance. Tapio Wirkkala's *Ultima Thule* has a personal appeal. Timo Sarpaneva's designs show another peak of perfection, with his glass sculptures striking uniquely Finnish notes. 'Pierced by the sun's shaft', the glass and stone centrepiece in Tampere city hall sticks in the memory of all who see it. Iittala, Karhula, Nuutajärvi remain magic names although designers should beware that for the sake of producing something new the result is not something ephemeral. Oiva Toikka has created objects of lasting appeal with his glass birds — crows, eider ducks, snow buntings — as well as with his wonderful 'senseless things' (as he calls his glass panels).

In the applied arts, an ability to bring 'the charm of novelty to things of everyday', as Coleridge happily expressed it, is regularly encountered. There spring to mind the polished bowls carved out of the swellings on birchtree trunks, the straw *himmeli* fashioned for Christmas decorations, the teapot and saucepan stands made out of hexagons of juniper wood, the ingenious Aarikka sheep conceived out of little balls of birchwood. Novelty and simplicity go together in much Finnish kitchenware. Many producers seem to have adopted the Finnish model for shaping the humble scissors (and was Fiskars the first to produce left-handed ones?). Homes as well as museums retain simple furniture from the old days. Empire-style chairs, settees and tables — legs chiselled or carefully turned, white or pastel-painted, with a touch of gilt — display a pleasing elegance. They belong to the days before springs — but Finland is still a country where the body is discouraged from sinking into seats. Long-case clocks, their durable if primitive mechanisms still working, their everyday cases decorated with simple floral designs, are another item to cherish. So too are the family *ryijy* wall hangings that have survived generations of moths, damp and fire, sober in their colouring from vegetable dyes.

It was perhaps necessary to run the gamut of Biedermeyer and worse before rising to the cultured simplicities of *Jugend* style furnishings and the eventual elegances of Alvar Aalto. The pliant birch, employed domestically since time immemorial, was to yield increasing potential as it passed through the plywood and veneer stages into the era of more subtle laminations that offered Aalto the opportunity to play his endless variations on the theme of the functional in furniture. His everyday chairs are its ultimate expressions.

Function and form have found a happy harmony in Finnish design. However, it is a harmony frequently founded on a strict discipline. Understandably, there has been a reaction, with the supporters of postmodernism seeking to escape from understatement, reticence and control.

How far liberation can explain another art form it is difficult to say. It was too much to expect that Finland could escape from the rash of urban graffiti that has sullied many cities of Europe. The bold and colourful spraygun frescoes, often executed with considerable talent, can be all right in the right place. In the wrong place, the joyous pop art that they represent is nothing more than pollution. The smooth surfaces of an increasing number of rock cuttings are defiled by copycat designs. No offence is greater when one reflects on the aesthetic attraction of granite itself, let alone the works of art that can be created from it.

Quite different are the enduring bronzes that are an integral part of the experience of those who walk the streets of Helsinki. Old friends include Eino Leino, a flamboyant figure about to stride down Helsinki's Esplanade, and the pensive Aleksis Kivi seated beside the National Theatre. Mannerheim is appropriately mounted, but the other presidents on parade look a little stilted in somewhat out-of-date suits. Yet perhaps they are more in keeping with the feelings of most Finns than the reduction of Paasikivi to a pair of stones symbolic of east and west. In their own special park the welded organ pipes with which Eila Hiltunen has paid tribute to Sibelius are an inspired gesture. *Havis Amanda*, with her playful sea creatures, is regarded with affection by the natives of Helsinki: so, too the *Three Smiths* who pursue their labours unperturbed by the daily *mêlée* of surrounding pedestrians. *Larin Paraske*, the rune singer, is a modest tribute to a legendary artist. Alexander II stands primly in the wide expanse of Senate Square. The romantic statue to *The Shipwrecked* on Observatory Hill immediately invites comparison with the solemn memorial to the victims of a lake steamer disaster on a bluff above Näsijärvi in Tampere. It is ironical that one of Tampere's *pièces de résistance* — totally unrelated to the shipwreck — is Eila Hiltunen's sculpture *Under Water*. Heikki Varja's tribute to Finnish literacy — *Sata vuotta uutisia* — sticks in the mind. Eager, satirical, humorous — it might be a sculpture of any three Tampere citizens enjoying a newspaper in Reima and Raili Pietilä's library before which is stands. Equally appealing are the wooden sculptures of Eva Ryynänen, her remarkable wooden chapel at Vuontislahti and the wall panelling at Unilever House in London.

Nor can the ephemeral contributions of Finland's poster artists be forgotten — and the rise of the Finnish graphics industry to which they owe so much. The Finnish Tourist Board is remembered for some of the most attractive wall posters to come out of the country. They look beyond the woods and the waters. Two are of the quintessence of the countryside. There is a bouquet of wild flowers gathered in a spendthrift summer by Erik Bruun (see the cover of this volume) and, complementarily, an autumn harvest of berries carpeting a patch of heath. Furthermore, for tourists who still send postcards, Finland must be unrivalled in its coverage of native flowers, fruits, birds, beasts, fishes and insects. For a whole gallery of cards, displaying a fidelity to lowly (and lovely) things, a debt is owed to the endeavours of the Finnish Naturalists Trust and to the

talented Helo family in Kajaani. The same qualities are found intermittently in the designs of Finnish postage stamps, which provide much
pleasure for philatelists whose collections are devoted to the world of
nature.

Words and music

The world of nature and of humble domesticity claim a considerable place
in the canon of Finnish literature — or at least in that part of it which is
accessible in one of the world languages. Such features are inseparable from
the considerable number of self-taught authors.

For many the introduction to Finland itself, as well as to Finnish
literature, has been by way of *Kalevala*. High drama and magical
adventurings may prevail, but much of *Kalevala* is also rooted in everyday
life and domesticity. It has elements of the Book of Genesis and of the
Book of Revelation. In it are many beginnings — an interpretation of the
geographical beginnings, of the colonial beginnings, of the beginnings of
Christianity. The primitive, orally transmitted poetry is in the *lingua sacra*
of the Finnish people, the language as it was before it assumed the form of
Biblical Finnish in the seventeenth century. For C.A. Gottlund, *Kalevala*
was 'the crystal in which nationality is mirrored'. The Irish poet Seamus
Heaney has identified a category of literary works that give 'access to an
evolutionary racial ear'. *Kalevala* belongs to it.

Before it was available in English translation, *Kalevala* appeared in
Swedish and German. The Oxford polyglot Max Müller encountered it
soon after and was one of the earliest foreigners to appreciate its epic
qualities. 'A Finn is not a Greek — Wäinämöinen is not a Homer', he
wrote, nevertheless '*Kalevala* possesses merits not dissimilar from those of
the *Iliad.*' Wider realisation of these qualities awaited an English rendering. Longfellow is presumed to have been familiar with Schiefner's German translation and to have derived from *Kalevala* the metrical form of
Hiawatha. Unexpectedly, the first English translation was made by the
American J.M. Crawford. Together with that of William Kirby, the
metrical form therefore struck a familiar chord in the English-speaking
world. More scholary translations, such as that of J. Francis Peabody
Magoun Jr, have succeeded those of Crawford and Kirby; there have also
been more poetic versions. Keith Bosley may have strayed from the straight
and narrow path of direct translation, but he has achieved a transformation
— indeed, a transfiguration — as only a poet can. He has invested
Kalevala with a lyrical radiance which adds to the attraction of the original.
What is more, he has used his skills on *Kanteletar* to equal effect.

Without translators, *Kalevala* — published in its proto form in 1835
and final form in 1849 — would remain a closed book to the outside

world. Without the inspiring example of Elias Lönnrot arranging the oral fragments that he so diligently collected, the publication of the rich *Kalevala* materials would certainly have been delayed. With the passage of time, purists have found grounds for disapproval of Lönnrot's methods of presentation, but the diligent doctor of medicine has triumphed over his critics. *Kalevala* is remembered with a special day in the Finnish calendar: on February 28 all flags fly.

The *Kalevala* characters and their experiences have inspired the entire Finnish artistic world. *Kalevala* has cried out for illustration, and the answer came from Akseli Gallen-Kallela. Karelian romanticist that he was, it was natural for him to seek out a model from the men of remote Kuhmo to replace the classical image of Orpheus and his lyre, with which R.W. Ekman had endowed Väinämöinen. The boldness, the vividness, the firebird colourings of Gallen-Kallela cast the illustrations of others in the shade. Joseph Alanen may offer a momentary challenge with, for example, *Lemminkäinen and the Great Snake*, but none of the Russian artists who have illustrated the Soviet editions of *Kalevala*, let alone cosmopolitans at large, has ever equalled the exuberant flights of Gallen-Kallela.

Similarly in the musical realm, one composer has dominated. Lauri Saikkola has his scenes from *Kalevala*, Tauno Marttinen has a series of *Kalevala* choral works, Uuno Klami has a *Kalevala Suite*; but from airy Luonnotar to mighty Kullervo, it is Jean Sibelius whose compositions prevail. Even in his fine incidental music for *The Tempest*, Ariel and Caliban somehow seem to become Luonnotar and Kullervo. And there are memories of a Sibelian score, largely bereft of appropriate tone poems, triumphant despite the exotically Ruritanian *Kalevala* conceived by Britain's Royal Ballet.

Finlandia, of course, is always triumphant, and personal experiences of it constantly recur — *Finlandia* in a bitterly cold King's College Chapel, in Cambridge, in January 1940 with Boris Ord at the organ and six regimental trumpeters to add effect; *Finlandia* adopted as a Welsh hymn tune; *Finlandia* at a Scottish funeral service. . . . The ninetieth birthday of Sibelius celebrated at Claridge's hotel in London with the Anglo-Finnish Society's dinner in 1955 with a speech by Sir Thomas Beecham (no notes, therefore no record, but the bravura of the delivery would be lost on paper). Malcolm Sargent did the honours for the centenary. A recording of the fifth Symphony was played after a long lunch with Arthur Wuorinen in New York in 1953. There is a memory of Liisa Linko braving the killing December fog of the same year to sing *Luonnotar*. Raymond Bantock was encountered at a dinner which continued with cloudberry liqueur in his mews apartment where he told of Sibelius's visits to his father, to whom the Third Symphony is dedicated. Rosa Newmarch acted as an interpreter on those occasions. Entirely coincidentally and for Norwegian reasons, the pleasure of a lunch at the Danish Club with Rosa Newmarch's daughter, turned into a productive Sibelian occasion. It was not difficult to persuade her to donate the letters that Sibelius had written to her mother to the Sibelius Museum. Erik Tawaststjerna is remembered for striking a chord of the Eighth Symphony during a lively Independence Day lecture at the University of London. Harriet Cohen claimed that she had the chord on a postcard (is it in the portmanteau of correspondence at the British Library to be opened in the presence of her executors in the year 2000?). The chord must be the ultimate in economy and elegance. Perhaps it was wrong to decline an opportunity to visit Ainola when Sibelius was alive, but it could only have been the intrusion of yet another stranger who had come to stare and had little to offer in return.

There are other Finnish musical experiences independent of those linked with Sibelius. They include memories of Astra Desmond singing the songs of Yrjö Kilpinen and of Elisabeth Söderström pulling out items from her Finnish repertoire. The neglected ballet music by Ahti Sonninen for *Pessi and Illusia* is recalled with much pleasure. Erkki Arni is remembered for his sensitive lectures on Finnish music, not least for introducing Aarre Merikanto's *Juha*. The romantic Toivo Kuula piano trio has unforgettable associations both with the former Arts Council drawing room at the Astor house in St. James's Square and with Kenwood orangery (not least for the nightmare of organising the transport of a Bechstein concert grand piano). Kuula's neglected work was a revelation; so, too, the clarinet concerto by the eighteenth-century Finn, Bernhard Crusell. Fredrik Pacius's *King Charles's Hunt*, Finland's first opera, was introduced by way of the libretto of Topelius before the pleasure of a recording was received from Pacius's granddaughter. *Piae Cantiones*, 'a gift from the island of Finland' as its subtitle says, is appealing fare for the many formidable lay choirs that strive to find audiences. How much richer Lutheran church services would be with such choirs. The age-old intoning by cleric or cantor, often near to the key rather than on it, is a condition scarcely improved by the use of the microphone. It is all in striking contrast to the choral liturgy of Saturday night Orthodox services.

Joonas Kokkonen's *Last Temptations* has proved a triumph in the Lutheran mode but, like Leevi Madetoja's *Ostrobothnians*, it is somewhat too Finnish to export save by a native ensemble. Memories of a highly successful production of Aulis Sallinen's *The King goes forth to France* at Covent Garden and the praise bestowed on *Kullervo* in Los Angeles suggest that an imaginatively conceived presentation of *The Red Line* might be timely. Helsinki's new opera house should inspire composers as well as offering further opportunities to the galaxy of Finnish talent that has joined the international musical circuit.

The late twentieth century has witnessed a blossoming of music in Finland. Summer music festivals have become powerful attractions — Kuhmo for chamber music, Kaustinen for folk music, Pori for jazz and Savonlinna for the international opera season. Meanwhile, the efforts that have gone into the establishment of municipal orchestras have steadily built up standards that merit the construction of new concert halls to meet their needs. And never in the history of the country have there been so many children's intrumental ensembles — which is where future performers and audiences are born.

It is all a far cry from the age of the *kantele*, the first encounter with which is inevitably memorable. It was shortly after the war in the one-time home of Juhani Aho, whose *Rautatie* is such an amiable novel. Since then, the *kantele* has enjoyed a revival in the classroom, with thousands of youthful fingers plucking its strings to more than tolerable effect, while for those who aspire to greater professionalism a special *kantele* school is to be found at Mekrijärvi in northern Karelia. With the *kantele* goes the fine legacy of folksongs (which recalls an occasion in Liverpool when Olavi Pesonen, an unexpected member of the audience, volunteered a selection of them). Folk dancing, inseparable from folksong, is a legacy enjoyed in common with the rest of the Nordic countries. It brings to mind summer days when the slightest excuse seems to be good enough for folk dance groups to bring out their costumes and present their repertory. At a personal level, the irresistible bounce of the Säkkijärvi polka, inevitably enlivened by one of those accordions which the Finns continue to make with such skill, had an immediate attraction. It was first danced cumbrously in a barn in Lapinlahti with the formidable *emäntä* of the local guest house. The polka is one of the rumbustious items that account for the popularity of Teuvo Pakkala's *Tukkijoella*, a kind of 1920s entertainment about the log-floating fraternity, in the intervals of which, in the staid vestibule of the National Theatre, members of the audience are invited to dance with the company.

Such musical exuberance is not without its frustrations. So much music is composed in present-day Finland that only rarely, if ever, is it likely to be performed frequently inside let alone outside the country. In addition, and as elsewhere, so much is composed which conforms to the canons of composition, which is elegant in its own terms but which fails to appeal to the mass of the concert-going public.

> *And now put ice in your music*
> *It'll turn to mathematics.*

Perhaps Eeva-Liisa Manner put her finger on the obstacle some time ago.

One difficulty recalls another. Endless attempts have been made to help British musical ensembles give a correct rendering of the Finnish National

Anthem — *Maamme/Vårt land.* 'What is that tune that is being played?', enquired a Finn as the company rose in the course of a dinner for the Finnish President at the Mansion House in London. Not for the first time, it seemed evident that the tempo proved too challenging for the average foreign band.

Music can speak universally, but to appreciate the literature of another country demands a thorough knowledge of the language. Translation is critical if Finnish literature is to reach an international audience, where the competition for readership is infinite. Moreover, because the proportion of books translated tends to diminish as a result of the ever-growing number of publications, the reader is only likely to encounter Finnish literature around the edges. Most of the books translated into a world language remain little known. Those that have achieved six-figure sales, with Mika Waltari heading the list, have not always dealt with Finnish subjects. And when a Finnish bestseller such as Väinö Linna's *Unknown Soldier* breaks through the language barrier, the limitations of its wartime perspectives become apparent beside the statements of Erich Maria Remarque, Robert Graves or Antoine de St-Exupéry with which it is inevitably compared.

Alex Matson's translation of *The Seven Brothers* introduced Aleksis Kivi to a world readership. It is an endearing book, the contents of which touch universals because they are rooted in the civilising process itself. Every reader will have a favourite passage. The encounter of the brothers 'stout as tree stumps' with their A-B-C books might have come from the pen of Thornton Wilder. Then again there is the dream of Eero that the country of his birth might no longer be 'a vague part of a vague world, of which he knew neither the location nor the character'. The urban counterpart to its lowly rural background is found in the proletarian novels of Toivo Pekkanen. It was an inspired choice of the *Nordic Translation Series* to turn to Pekkanen's *My Childhood* — memoirs which reflect the lean and hungry mood of the early days of Finnish independence. Pekkanen is unforgettable as he recuperates from illness through the radiance of Christmas — a Finnish Tiny Tim.

Personal literary encounters are necessarily fortuitous. Juhani Aho's *Lastuja* was acquired in a French translation — *Copeaux.* Since F.E. Sillanpää has been the most widely translated Finnish novelist, it is natural to have been weaned on him, if not exactly wooed by him. Contrastingly, Tove Jansson's Moomintrolls immediately wooed, although a zoologist would have to admit that the Moomins as they are illustrated appear to have a biology more appropriate to the sub-tropical than to the sub-arctic. Because it became available in French there is a feeling that Joel Lehtonen's earthy *Putkinotko* ought to have Zolaesque qualities. The conclusion of *Jooseppi of Ryysyranta* is difficult to forget. And, thanks to the periodical *Books from Finland*, the appetite is constantly whetted by regular excerpts from contemporary Finnish literature in translation. Will the English-speaking world ever be able to enjoy to the full Leena Krohn's *Umbra* (and the 'paradox archive') or Lars Sund's *Colorado Avenue* as it is able to relish Bo Carpelan's *Axel*?

It is not easy to avoid the poems of J.L. Runeberg because of his highly recitable *Tales of Ensign Stål*, full of 'old forgotten far-off things and battles long ago'. The *Tales* have yet to be translated well. There are recollections of extracts being declaimed in the original Swedish by Jacob von Julin at an Anglo-Finnish supper party in the 'Prospect of Whitby', a London 'East End' pub overlooking the Thames, as well as of the first reading by John Benn of his translation of *Sven Dufva*, the best to date, given at a Runeberg evening at the old Swedish Chamber of Commerce off Trinity Square. The *Tales* are fixed in the mind by the illustrations of Albert Edelfelt, especially that of 'The March of the Björneborg Men', which is in the Gösta Serlachius collection at Mänttä — and which recalls in turn the hospitality received there while investigating the early archives of the paper company.

To have been guided line by line through Eino Leino's *Helkavirsiä* and the text of *Tarquinius Superbus* before going to a production at the National Theatre were experiences not likely to be forgotten. The same applies to the domestic dramas of Minna Canth, sending thoughts scurrying back to Kuopio where, as she presided over her country store, her fertile imagination was doubtless able to benefit from the anecdotes heard as she went about her daily business.

Literature in Swedish being more personally accessible, there was an early encounter with two poems of Elmer Diktonius — *The Machine* and *The Jaguar* (for all its revolutionary overtones, suddenly recalling William Blake's *Tiger*):

> *Sunspots dance —*
> *all whirls nimbly.*
> *With a laugh*
> *the jaguar hurls himself over*
> *the top of the fir trees —*
> *Hear the star-laughter in its roar.*

Given its range and volume, the foreigner must also be grateful to Thomas Warburton for providing a readable rollcall of contemporary Finnish literature in the Swedish language, to authorities such as George Schoolfield for providing specialist appraisals, and to translators such as David McDuff and Joan Tate.

For most foreigners in Finland, paint on canvas is more readily appreciated than words on paper. As always, what appeals is a matter of personal

taste and sometimes of casual encounter. There are paintings that disturb
— Tyko Sallinen's *Hihhulit* or Hugo Simberg at his most macabre and
symbolic. There are paintings that attract because of their quiet Finnish
character, especially Pekka Halonen's winter studies and Ellen Thesleff's
impressionistic masterpieces. There are unexpected portraits — Gallen-
Kallela's Gustav Mahler. There are paintings that are fun — Juho
Rissanen's *The Fortune Teller* and the Lapp primitives. Illustrators of
childrens' books such as Mauri Kunnas ought to have an international
appeal. Paintings out of context often make a greater impact. To be confronted with one of Reidar Särestöniemi's brilliantly colourful canvases
in the *Kaleva* newspaper office meant more than seeing another in Urho
Kekkonen's Tamminiemi. To find two of the many haunting and discreetly
coloured self-portraits of Helene Schjerfbeck looking out from a collection
of Scandinavian paintings at Sotheby's saleroom in Bond Street was to
realise the stature of her work (how Virginia Woolf, Vanessa Bell or Edith
Sitwell would have doted on them).

Quirky paintings have made their mark, none more so than the portrait
of Daniel Kajanus, the Lapland giant immortalised by Enoch Seeman, all
eight feet of him plus a turban. His abnormal height gained Kajanus a place
in the entourage of King Augustus II of Poland, and in 1734 this 'prodigy
of nature' from Kainuu was to be viewed at half-a-crown a time in
London's Great Suffolk Street. For long the portrait hung, seemingly
inconsequentially, at Boughton House near Kettering or at Dalkeith near
Edinburgh from where the Duke of Buccleuch (owner of both houses),
probably bemused by his possession, sold it in 1975 so that Daniel might be
more appropriately hung in the National Museum of Finland.

Buying and selling recalls the changing value of works of art. In the
immediate post-war years, von Wright bird paintings were to be bought
in Kensington Church Street for the proverbial song. Two generations
later, and set in a Scandinavian context, bids for selected Finnish paintings
reached five and six figures in London's West End auction rooms.

The art of patronage

The arts and the sciences in Finland are heavily indebted to public spon-
sorship and private patronage. For a foreigner there always seems to be
money available for their promotion. The Academy of Finland is a primary
source of funding, there are special institutions for helping technical
research, at the individual level there are state grants for young artists of
promise, and ministries never seem to be at a loss to obtain support for
Finnish cultural events abroad.

Finland may lack charitable foundations on the scale of the world's
richer nations because, when oil barons, railway kings and industrialists

were accumulating the wealth that enabled them to establish their endow-
ments, Finnish manufacturing was still in the chrysalis stage. Nevertheless,
there is a variety of modest foundations which bear the names of public-
spirited entrepreneurs, the awards from which are coveted as much for the
honour that they bring as for the financial assistance. Thus, names such as
Kordelin and Wihuri ring bells for graduates with research proposals,
while Oxford, Cambridge, London and Edinburgh have welcomed gradu-
ate students for a generation thanks to be benefactions of Oskari
Huttunen. Picture galleries also bear testimony to the generosity of
donors. Beyond the collections of the carefully restored Ateneum in
Helsinki, there are unexpected treasures in Turku and Vaasa, while the
Sara Hildén gallery in Tampere is remembered as a jewel in the crown.

There may be political arguments about the direction of expenditure, as
in all local government circles, but in Finland it is always civic pride that
seems to triumph. Architecture is regarded as something of a celebration,
with the extravagant gesture triumphant and eventually applauded. It may
be a place of entertainment, such as the Finnish Theatre in Turku, or
simply a water tower, with a town such as Jakobstad employing Lars
Sonck to design it. It may equally be the support given to a project such as
fills the Nokia Cable factory at Kerava, redundant space being made over
the 'creative chaos' of a host of artistic enterprises, with a spacious gallery
which will be recalled for an exhibition of heroic frescoes by Lennart
Segerstråle.

Civic pride is complemented by civic hospitality, and by the standards of
most countries that of the Finns is rarely exceeded. As a result, they have
acquired a reputation as hosts for conferences. Largely because of its
location and its neutral stance, Finland has had the experience of
accommodating major East-West meetings — and, whatever the out-
come of the revolutionary changes that mark the close of the twentieth
century, it will continue to offer an attractively detached setting for such
gatherings.

Simultaneously, the Union of International Associations indicates that
Finland hosts well over 100 conferences annually. The 30,000 members of
professional organisations who assemble in Finland may in most years raise
eyebrows at the comparative costs, but in retrospect memories will be of
the efficiency with which their gatherings were conducted and of the
generous patronage of their hosts. At the same time, civic rivals who
succeed in attracting conference organisers to use their facilities must
sometimes look at their balance sheets and question how much financial
gain accrues to their local taxpayers. Contrastingly, there is little doubt
that where seedcorn has been sown by local patrons and sponsors in
festivals, especially of the arts, the harvests have yielded returns a
hundredfold.

8

GREAT EXPECTATIONS

Jag ser för konstens hand dess söners snille sprida
Liksom dess bergs granit, en oförmoden glans:
Och Finland lyft vid Sveriges sida,
Beundras af en verld, som glömde att det fanns. *
(Finlands uppodling, *Åbo Tidning*, 1, 1800)

Fin de siècle

If there is one condition from which Finland does not appear to suffer it is
fin de sièclisme. The last decade of the eighteenth century was one of
considerable enterprise and lively anticipation. Although its effects were
limited geographically, the intellectual atmosphere in the old capital and
the practical measures initiated by its citizens merited the epithet *Åbo
anima regni*. The end of the nineteenth century witnessed a blossoming
across the entire artistic field, and this ran parallel with and in many cases
was inseparable from the remarkable resistance to Russian pressure. In
addition, it marked the beginning of a changed role for women in society.
During the 1990s, side by side with the stimulus deriving from a wider and
deeper interest in the past, there has been an unequalled concern with the
future. In each of these three decades the provincial experience, the
national experience and the international experience have manifested distinctive qualities.

With the dawn of the 1990s, the relaxation of tension in Europe and the
high standard of living at home created a buoyant mood among Finns. In
fact from the standpoint of the 1940s, Finland had reached the promised
land. As it approached the fourth generation of its independence, it had
become a country of superfluities. Ironically, having escaped from what
Edwin Muir would have called the 'treadmill problems' set by the physical
environment, it was to be confronted with a disturbing new set of problems born of economic and financial factors. Moreover, they were basic to
the framework of international trading within which Finland had been
operating so effectively.

During the third generation of its independence, Finland's international
network of commercial contacts had been transformed. London provided
evidence of it. Finland House in Haymarket was a shopwindow in the
1960s. Its offices housed a handful of leading Finnish companies, and its

---

*I can see the genius of its sons spreading light through their art in the same way as its granite rocks
can shine unexpectedly, and Finland, taking off by Sweden's side, admired by a world once
unaware of its existence.

sauna and club enjoyed a passing success. However, the premises, regarded as prestigious in their day, soon became inadequate, and today the official Finland Trade Centre in Pall Mall flies the flag. It provides information for and about the hundreds of Finnish agencies and representatives that are widely scattered throughout the United Kingdom. An independent Finnish-British Trade Guild also fosters links. To move from the West End to the City of London is to encounter the signs of most of Finland's financial houses. One bank is lodged in the historic Deanery of St Paul's, the first residence to be built in the City after the Great Fire. Signs also indicate that the London offices are matched by others in Frankfurt and Paris, New York and Zurich, even in Singapore and the Cayman Islands. In view of the number of these institutions, it is not surprising to learn that a substantial percentage of Finnish investment outside the country is in the financial sector.

Widespread restructuring of industry on the home front, with all its investment requirements, must have absorbed most if not all domestic saving. Accordingly, the presence of Finnish representatives in the international money markets has been critical in attracting foreign capital for the multinational enterprises built up by Finns over the last generation.

To have turned the pages of the *Bank of Finland Bulletin* regularly since before the Second World War and to have read the economic review *Unitas* for the last generation is to have followed (in their excellent English) the transformation of the Finnish financial system. It is to have become aware of the development of Helsinki's Stock Exchange, observed the caution with which restraints and restrictions on financial dealings have been relaxed, seen the emergence of monitoring systems as legislation had advanced and, latterly, witnessed the impact of recession on the behaviour of the familiar graphs that have long illustrated the *Bulletin* and *Unitas*.

The increase of investment in research and development reflects a healthy discourse between technocrats, economists and ecologists. To the outside observer it has rapidly become clear that Finland enjoys a number of advantages over many countries. First, it does not suffer the same degree of obsolescence as old-established industrial nations. Secondly, techno-philia prevails. Finland has space and, lean though much of it may be, there is no telling what undeveloped resources might be made accessible through the discovery and application of new techniques. Again, while its terri-torial extent and small population enable it to accommodate the litter resulting from twentieth-century industrial development, it has been exciting to see the effort devoted to programmes of waste disposal. The promotion of water recycling and energy conservation, the develop-ment of degradable products and the assault on pollution (especially in connection with softwood processing) are both practical and visionary. It is disturbing — and ironical — to see the recycling of waste paper in

Finland's traditional West European markets threatening its paper indus-try. Contrastingly, it is a pleasure to have seen the passing of the age when bottles, cans, cardboard boxes, packing cases and waste food were hurled over the sterns of Baltic ferries to the waiting gulls. The unpleasant flotsam and jetsam of the packaging economy that litters the Finnish shoreline has been correspondingly reduced.

Investment in research and development and the tenacity with which social, economic and ecological problems are tackled has helped to build a reputation abroad. Not least, it has influenced the opinions of those con-cerned with assessing the stability of nations. Finland's late twentieth-century trajectory has been closely followed by international investment agencies. It is perhaps too much to expect that the Triple A of their ratings (a status awarded to only six other countries) can be maintained indefi-nitely, but the very fact that it has been attainable is a stimulus to constant effort.

'The singer will turn back to his beloved shadows. For the scientist, time and light lie before,' wrote Aldous Huxley in *Adonis and the Alphabet*. In Finland, as elsewhere, the applied scientist and the social scientist, like the physical scientist, look to a future in which they can see the fulfilment of their theories and experiments. At the same time, as the humanist knows, to turn back is to see more than 'the beloved shadows'. It is to see the present and future in fuller perspective. The wheels of fortune painted on the walls of Finland's medieval churches have a message for today no less than in the past. In the midst of material achievements and great expectations, they serve to remind Finns of worldly uncertainties.

With increasing internationalisation, the impact of external forces upon Finland has become more powerful, more widely distributed and swifter in its effects that hitherto. At the same time, there has been a shift of emphasis from the politico-military imperatives that dominated so much of Finnish policy-making for so long to socio-economic pressures. In the course of two generations, Finns have lived fearing the worst of fates and have tasted the best in life. When there is a downturn in their fortunes, memories of past anxieties have a habit of gathering around events like St Elmo's fire. *Inconstantia mundi* — more than most peoples, Finns are haunted by the fickleness of life. As the familiar is transformed into the unfamiliar they must find their way, metaphorically, around a new map of Europe — indeed, a new map of the world.

Finland beyond Finland

If the world has overlooked the transformation of Finland there is no overlooking the Finns themselves. Today they are sufficiently ubiquitous for it to be asked if the national population can really be only five millions.

There were, of course, peoples of Finnish origin and related Fínno-Ugrians beyond Finland long before Finns entered the international stream of migrants. There have always been propulsive and attractive forces encouraging movement. The personal experience of Finland is extended by encountering Finns and Finnish connections in other lands.

Along the Swedish-Norwegian border country in the province of Värmland it is easy to imagine that one is in eastern Finland. Farmers from Savo and Karelia were encouraged to settle here in the sixteenth and seventeenth centuries and to open up the uninhabited frontier territories. The descendants of the Finnish pioneers were half-forgotten until the ethnographer C.A. Gottlund reported on their neglected condition during his early nineteenth-century travels (Gottlund's papers in the archive of the National Museum indicate an interest in all Finns beyond Finland from the shores of the Caspian to the banks of the Delaware). Finnskogarna, as the border area is known today, is a source of curiosity for anyone interested in the Finnish diaspora. The legacy of Finnish placenames remains firmly on the contemporary map, Finnish artifacts have been assembled in local museums (where there may be custodians with Finnish names who know nothing of the Finnish language and little of Finland itself), and the Finnish element is cultivated by tourist agencies as a distinctive feature of the Värmland inheritance.

Beyond Finland's northern frontiers, there are other areas long settled by Finns. Settlement west of the Tornio river in Swedish Norrland was well established when Linnaeus journeyed to Lapland in 1737. The descendants of the settlers are tenacious of the Finnish language and differ from the politically radical migrants who moved across the border in response to the needs of Swedish mining and forestry. Travel by early morning bus from Luleå to Haparanda, and the driver will speak Swedish until he takes coffee at Kalix or Sangis after which he will change to Finnish in response to his passengers' needs. Not surprisingly there has been pressure — and successful pressure — for the employment of Finnish as the language of instruction in schools in the eleven Swedish parishes where it is regularly spoken. Although the circumstances are different, a Finnish minority problem exists in the north Norwegian counties of Finnmark and Troms. Finns have migrated to Finnmark — Ruija, as they call it — for centuries, driven out of their home areas by famine and attracted by the prospect of food from a more generous sea. The Finnish element is scattered principally around the fringes of Varangerfiord and the Varanger peninsula. It has Norwegian citizenship, but to encounter it is to sense something of a dual patrimony. Finnish names have been planted on the land. The language persists. In the past, at least, Finns have given rise to a substantial literature about the challenge that they have represented to Norwegian authority.

To the south-east, after 1809, Finns had access to the territories of the
Russian empire and a steady stream of migrants moved across the border.
Their talents were employed in the service of Russia as administrators
(including the governorship of Alaska), as officers in the armed services
(John Screen has written about them), as merchants and entrepreneurs
(some of whom helped to open up Siberia), as academics and artisans. At
the turn of the century, St Petersburg and the surrounding administrative
area had about the same number of Finns born in Finland as Minnesota and
Michigan. As a major city, St Petersburg provided a valuable market for
Finnish products, especially for the farming community that had access to
it (how curious in the late twentieth century to visit Lapinlahti dairy and to
find lorry loads of surplus dried milk making for the same outlet). The rise
of interest by Finnish historians in the Finnish community of St Petersburg
has opened up entertaining areas of research (Max Engman identifying the
near monopoly of Finnish chimney sweeps is an amusing example). The
prior inhabitants of the area — the forgotten Ingrians — have also
claimed attention. Is the presence of the Ingrians one reason why so many
familiarly Finnish faces are so often to be seen in the streets of present-day
St Petersburg?

Finns in the merchant navy are in some ways resident beyond their
homeland. There is a long tradition of seagoing among the coastal Finns.
Like the Norwegians, they entered the late nineteenth century carrying
trade with their modest cooperatively-owned vessels, escaping to open
waters when winter closed the Baltic Sea, eventually creating legends with
their fleet of tall ships.

Finnish emigrants to the New World followed in the wake of the
Scandinavians. As church records and passport applications attest, they left
in large numbers from Ostrobothnia. At the peak of their movement,
emigrant ships brought them from Hangö to Hull, from where they
crossed to Liverpool to take steerage passages on the fleet of trans-Atlantic
steamships. Those who were not caught in the urban nets of the eastern
seaboard of the United States, moved principally to the residual lands of the
upper Middle West. There are memories of personal encounters with
Ostrobothnians in the small declining mill towns of New England and
with unexpected clusters of Finnish farmers whose parents filled the gaps
left by Scandinavian settlers on the good soils of southern Minnesota.
North shore Lake Superior is recalled as Saturday smoke-sauna country,
identifiably Finnish independently of the family names on the roadside
letterboxes. Hancock and Suomi College are remembered, hard by the
Copper Peninsula (Kuparinsaari) of upstate Michigan: so too are the
Finnish tombstones side by side with those of the Cornish miners who
preceded them.

The lesser stream of Finns who crossed the Atlantic to the Canadian and

American shores of the northern Great Lakes after the Civil War of
1917–18 are recalled for their radical reputations. From the perspectives of
the late twentieth century, it is curious to cast an eye over the 'Red'
newspapers that they published in the Iron Range country of Minnesota
and the nickel and cobalt towns of Ontario. For a long time, in cities such
as Toronto, the Finnish communities displayed paler versions of the polar-
ities that divided society in the homeland — social clubs were coloured by
political allegiances: church congregations by degrees of evangelism. Suspicion hung about the Finnish population in Canada even during the Second
World War. It took fully a generation for the image to change. Slowly
Canadians discovered Finland for themselves and exchanged formal diplomatic representation. The energies of the Canadian Friends of Finland, the
diligent labours of historians such as Pirkko Lindström of the University
of Toronto, together with prestigious links such as Finnair's Montreal
route and the winning Finnish design for Toronto City Hall, have transformed the Canadian picture of Finland.

Finnish emigrants have included their share of idealists and adventures
who have looked for great expectations beyond the seas. A handful of
fortune seekers were lured to the goldfields of South Africa and Australia.
Utopias were sought in the Pampas of the Argentine, in Brazil's Penedo,
in the Pacific islands, in the western Avernus of America. Edith Södergran
caught the mood —

> Somewhere a long way off in a far land
> There is a bluer sky and a wall with roses
> And a palm and a milder wind
> And that is all.

The Finns of the diaspora, past and present, are brought to life in the
pages of *Suomen silta*, the journal of *Suomi Seura*, which strives to bridge
the gap between those at home and those abroad. And the Finns who have
left their homeland are grist to the mill of the Institute of Migration at
Turku, where a data bank is being built up from individual records and the
movements of emigrants can be conjured up on bright computer screens. It
is yet another haunt for ancestor-hunters.

Occasionally, Finns embrace a new citizenship and make their reputation in adopted lands. Westwards, the House of Commons in London
benefited from the good fortune that led Konni Zilliacus and Patrick
Donner — the left hand and right hand of the parliamentary lobby — to
choose British citizenship. Eastwards, O.W. Kuusinen contrived to live a
full life in the Soviet Union and to retain high office (Is it too fanciful to
suggest that in other circumstances, he might have been a not
undistinguished poet? There are memories of his bright, sharp daughter, as
smart a guest as any seen at a London party).

Once upon a time, those who left Finland rarely had the opportunity to return. In any case, perhaps Eino Leino's

> *Isänmaa, kotipaikka ja lies*
> *Puolue, perhe ja muu.* *

had little meaning for them. Their children's children can now make regular pilgrimages to the wellnigh unrecognisable homeland of their grandparents, while present-day Finns who choose to retire to foreign lands — and there are plenty of Finnish expatriates along the shores of the Mediterranean — are rarely more than a few hours from their home country.

A European presence

Finland is accustomed to balancing the consequences of its West European orientation and its East European location. It is both its fortune and misfortune that Finland has always been significant for Russia's profile in the rest of Europe. Partly for this reason, Finland has had to pay a price for its European inheritance.

Fundamental changes in the relations between Eastern and Western Europe would appear to offer considerable opportunities for Finland, but they carry with them the need to make fundamental adjustments in the economic sector. In respect of transport, Finland benefits from its geographical location. Although there are only three formal crossing points, transport quotas between Finland and Russia are unique in that they include permits for third parties. Goods therefore move relatively easily. Contrastingly, the restructuring of Russia inevitably disturbs the *status quo*. The practice of dealing with a unitary system and with highly centralised controlling agencies must be replaced by the establishment of a complex network of connections with the constituent parts of whatever loose confederation emerges. More important, the requirement to pay in hard currency for the critical sources of imported energy makes financial demands which any trade recession exacerbates. Finland has much to offer the lagging economies of its eastern neighbours, having had more practical experience than possibly any other country. Their management may not always have been easy, but a diversity of joint undertakings may be cited — from heavy engineering activities, through the refurbishment of historic buildings to the silvicultural surveys that will provide Russia with its first reliable information about a key resource. Finland's expertise in joint ventures recalls the guide through the Russian commercial maze provided in English by Matti Honkanen — a book personally relished in a

---

*Fatherland, home and hearth/Party, family and the rest. . .

mahogany-panelled room in *Pohjolan talo*, with wise owls gazing down from the ceiling. Joint enterprises with Estonia are correspondingly straightforward, with the 80 km across the Finnish Gulf lively with ferries and no longer, in the phrase of Jan Kaplinski, 'broad as an ocean'.

The fuller integration of the southern and eastern shores of the Baltic with those of the west and north strengthens Finland's position. The days of the Hanseatic League have been recalled, but a unitary and liberated Eastsea trading network through a Council of Baltic Sea states offers more than the prospect of a *Hansa rediviva*. The operations of the state-owned oil and chemical corporation, Neste, illustrate the potential for wider integration, with its plans for a series of service stations round the eastern and southern rim of the Baltic, the acquisition of North Sea oil and gas interests, and the long-term projects for developing — jointly with Norway, Sweden and Russia — the Barents Sea natural gas deposits.

It is ironic that the dramatic transformation of Eastern Europe should coincide with the submission by Finland of an application to join the European Economic Community. The Finnish economy has always been linked primarily with the markets of Western Europe. In anticipation of the increasing integration of the Community, Finnish manufacturers have invested heavily in the leading member states. The objectives have been to produce goods as near as possible to the market in order to focus on local strengths, avoid rising domestic labour costs and escape as far as possible high Finnish interest rates. Furthermore, to benefit from the knowledge-based technologically developed industries that Finland is creating so successfully, a broader field of operations is needed.

While Finland has gained much through its commercial assertiveness in the market of the Community, it has been apprehensive about political absorption by it. It has been well aware of the 'small country squeeze' exerted by large political units — 'Portugalisation', as it has come to be known. And Finns know that the population of Portugal is three times that of their own country. The long-term spectre of pooled sovereignty has been seen as a threat; so, too, has the short-term destabilisation of the domestic economy. Agriculturalists have been especially sensitive about the likely challenge to the financial support that they receive. Contrastingly, with welfare provision in some ways ahead of that of the Community itself, a prospective social chapter would be unlikely to raise difficulties.

Reaction against membership has been instinctive for the majority. Once again metaphors have been generated. For Tuomas Nevanlinna, Europe has been 'the great Other', destined to save or to swallow Finland. Gunn Gestrin has seen Finland putting up a fence around its kitchen garden in the face of the Community. Others have considered Finland to be waiting in the vestibule, seeking out the tolerances in the system, hoping that the principle of exceptions will gain ground to their advantage and that the concept of subsidiarity can be clarified for their benefit. Markku Tykkyläinen has written of 'the periphery syndrome'. Finland's location on the circumference of the continent — *i kontinentens utkant* — is not without its geographical and psychological consequences, but the Community does not operate according to the concentric model conceived by von Thünen — or even that of Dante.

The Finnish presence in Europe is more than commercial: likewise the historic European presence in Finland. In the applied arts, to the common advantage of all and often under a Nordic banner, Finland continues to make its mark. Cities as far apart as Stockholm and Vienna, Kiruna, Wolfsberg and Essen have been enriched by its architectural contributions. The Milan *Triennale* has been a happy hunting ground for Finns; Cannes has honoured their films. Musically, it has been unnecessary for Finland to seek an audience or for most of its artists to search for contracts. All are expressions of what Paul Valéry called the power of radiation which is a distinctive quality of the countries of Europe no less than of Europe at large.

Europe is also alive with Finnish students. There have never been so many in European places of learning. The European Community Action Scheme for the Mobility of Students (Erasmus) will multiply their numbers and probably bring more European students to Finnish universities than hitherto. Simultaneously, Finland is multiplying its own institutes abroad. The renowned Villa Lante in Rome and the Athens Institute are complemented by the *Institut Finlandais* in Paris and the Finnish Institute in London (When will Berlin or Munich acquire a counterpart?). 'To experience difference . . . is to re-examine identity', wrote George Steiner in *After Babel*. Through their wider experiences in the countries of Europe, Finns have acquired broader perspectives. At the same time, they have come to appreciate more fully the quality of life at home. They must realise the advantages of being citizens of a country with a small population and space in which they can lose themselves as well as express themselves.

To have experienced the passage of two generations in Finland is to have witnessed fundamental shifts in the European relationship. With every move that has relaxed the geopolitical division of the continent, Finland, on the margins of the continent and with a virtually closed frontier to the east, has become a country of greater interest. Paradoxically, the reopening of the east intensifies Finland's links with the west because of the increasing number of travellers who enjoy the amenities it has to offer as they use it as a stepping stone on their journeys to and from the new Commonwealth of Independent States. More important, as a result of its technical transformation and ingenuity Finland, which was long at the receiving end of Western Europe, has become a contributor to Western Europe. Fifty years ago, a traveller to Finland often felt as if stepping back into the past of Western Europe. Today, in so many ways and despite the bewilderment that Finns often sense as they attempt to harmonise their relations with the European Community and the eastern Commonwealth, visitors from Western Europe can sometimes have the pleasant sensation that they are walking into the future.

'A little brief authority'

Expectations are always too great. Through the years there has been the expectation that it would be possible to keep abreast of most that was going on in Finland in the areas of personal interest and to communicate something of it to the English-speaking world. However, to keep an eye on publication alone has become a physical as well as a mental impossibility. The sheer number of new books encountered on regular visits to book fairs, the Academic Bookshop and Suomalainen Kirjakauppa is daunting. It has been a matter of furtively scanning a few pages with notebook in hand, writing down titles and then suffering a guilt complex for buying so little and wondering who has the money to purchase even a fraction of the temptations displayed. As for the multiplicity of journals and periodicals, there are always some that suddenly announce themselves having eluded observation sometimes through years. There must be many Finns who will recognise the problem.

Such a situation can easily inhibit publication, since academic bibliographies can never be complete. Hesitation to commit personal impressions to paper has different roots. It springs partly out of Jörn Donner's comment that perhaps the less written about his country by outsiders the better. More fundamentally, it is a reaction to the aphorism of Claude Lévi-Strauss that 'When we make an effort to understand, we destroy the object of our attachment.' Perhaps it is better not to try to 'unweave the rainbow'.

Yet it is wrong not to share experiences. There have been unexpected people who have known a remarkable amount about Finland, but who have left no record. They include the scores of teacher secretaries who have worked in Finland, most of whom ought to have something to contribute. They might have emulated Diana Ashcroft's memoir from Kajaani: they might have contributed autobiographical chapters such as those of James Bramwell. Possibly better still, an editor might have coaxed out of a group of them a book of essays. Perhaps prospective authors have heeded the fate of those who have been outspoken in their opinions and have had coals of fire heaped upon thier heads (but what fun an unabashed critic such as Neil Hardwick can be).

Time protects a favoured few from critical comment. No one will be able to read for thirty years the reports sent by diplomats from Helsinki to

Whitehall — and for even longer those sent to Helsinki by Finnish diplomats accredited abroad. It has been a privilege to know a succession of representatives of the Foreign and Commonwealth Office and the British Council who have served in Finland. Most of them, in their retirement, have expressed openly the attachment they formed for Finland during their years in office — the kind of attachment accorded to few other countries. Reciprocally, there are memories of the stream of Finnish diplomats who have obviously enjoyed their London postings and opened their hearts as well as their homes. Most cups run over in Finnish company: so much more is received than can be given.

There is one group of expatriates who have given more than they have received and whom only posterity can adequately reward. It consists of the unusually gifted group of translators from Finnish to English. The older generation includes David Barrett, Philip Binham, Malcolm Hicks, Herbert Lomas and John Atkinson, and they have anticipated a virtual school of no less competent younger British scholars — for scholars they are. It has been a pleasure to profit from the results of their talents and their company.

Every country is a Never-Never Land. What A.N. Whitehead has called 'the flux of the experienced world' suggests that it can only be captured momentarily and never permanently grasped. Ultimately, whatever is written about any country can be but the nodding acquaintance of a passer by

> Dressed in a little brief authority
> Most ignorant of what he's most assured.

INDEX